Political Parties

CORE DOCUMENTS

Political Parties

~ CORE DOCUMENTS ~

Selected and Introduced by

Eric C. Sands

ASHBROOK PRESS

Copyright © 2019 Ashbrook Center, Ashland University

Library of Congress Cataloging-in-Publication Data
Political Parties: Core Documents
Selected and Introduced by Eric Sands
   p.   cm.
Includes Index
1. United States—Politics and government.
ISBN 978-1-878802-48-4 (pbk.)

Cover images, above the title, left to right:
George Washington, Athenaeum portrait (photograph of Gilbert Stuart
   painting), Detroit Publishing Company, ca. 1900–1912. Library of
   Congress Prints and Photographs Division, LC-DIG-det-4a26084.
Former President Martin Van Buren, half-length portrait, facing
   right, photographed between 1840 and 1862. Library of Congress
   Prints and Photographs Division, LC-USZ62-13008.
G. W. Plunkitt, ca. 1910–1915. George Grantham Bain Collection, Library of
   Congress Prints and Photographs Division, LC-DIG-ggbain-14747.
Woodrow Wilson, ca. 1919. Library of Congress Prints and Photographs
   Division Washington, D.C., LC-USZC2-6247.
Senator George McGovern, photographed by Warren K. Leffler, June 30, 1972.
   Library of Congress Prints and Photographs Division, LC-DIG-ppmsca-19602.

Cover image, below the title:
"Grand procession of Wide-Awakes at New York on the evening of
   October 3, 1860," Wallach Division Picture Collection, October 13, 1860.
   Lincoln-Hamlin Campaign, Printing-House Square (Park Row and
   Nassau St.). New York Public Library Digital Collections, b17613364.

Interior design/composition: Brad Walrod/Kenoza Type, Inc.

Ashbrook Center at Ashland University
401 College Avenue
Ashland, Ohio 44805
www.ashbrook.org

ABOUT THE ASHBROOK CENTER

The Ashbrook Center restores and strengthens the capacities of the American people for constitutional self-government. Ashbrook teaches students and teachers across our country what America is and what she represents in the long history of the world. Offering a variety of resources and programs, Ashbrook is the largest university-based educator in the enduring principles and practice of free government. Dedicated in 1983 by President Ronald Reagan, the Ashbrook Center is governed by its own board and responsible for raising all of the funds necessary for its many programs.

BRING THE DOCUMENTS AND DEBATES OF THE NATION'S PAST INTO THE PRESENT

Readers of this volume may be particularly interested in Ashbrook's Teaching American History programs which provide an opportunity for secondary educators to explore themes in American history and self-government through the study of original historical documents. Designed especially for teachers, our seminar-style programs are offered online and on location, both on our campus and at sites around the country. We use discussions, not lectures and texts, not textbooks so that each seminar is a conversation among peers in which each attendee is an active participant in learning.

For more information, please visit us online at Ashbrook.org, TeachingAmericanHistory.org, and ReligionInAmerica.org.

Contents

Illustrations follow page 112

General Editor's Introduction

This collection of documents on political parties continues the Ashbrook Center's extended series of document collections covering major periods, themes and institutions in American history and government. The volume begins with James Madison's commentary on the unavoidable but dangerous nature of parties; it ends with the Supreme Court's opinion about the legitimate sources of funding for political party activities in *Citizens United*. It covers not only the developing role of political parties in our constitutional order, but also the specific answers given by various parties to important political questions over the course of our national history. Its documents also explore the leadership structures of political parties and especially the connection between party leadership and the presidency. This collection and its companion volumes—*The American Presidency, The Congress, The Judicial Branch, The Separation of Powers,* and *Federalism*—will comprise a detailed account of America's major political ideas and institutions. The document volume series will also include a collection of the most important Supreme Court decisions, as well as two volumes on the First Amendment. One will cover religious freedom and the other the freedoms of speech and assembly.

When the series of Ashbrook document collections is complete, it will be comprehensive as well as authoritative because it will present America's story in the words of those who wrote it—America's presidents, labor leaders, farmers, philosophers, industrialists, politicians, workers, explorers, religious leaders, judges, soldiers; its slaveholders and abolitionists; its expansionists and isolationists; its reformers and stand-patters; its strict and broad constructionists; its hard-eyed realists and visionary utopians—all united in their commitment to equality and liberty, yet all also divided often by their different understandings of these most fundamental American ideas. The documents are about all this—the still unfinished American experiment with self-government.

As this volume does, each of the volumes in the series will contain key documents on its period, theme, or institution, selected by an expert and reviewed by an editorial board. Each volume will have an introduction highlighting key documents and themes. In an appendix to each volume, there will also be a thematic table of contents, showing the connections between various documents. Another appendix will provide study questions for each document, as well as questions that refer to other documents in the collection, tying them together as the thematic table of contents does. Each document will be checked against an authoritative original source and have an introduction outlining its significance. Notes to each document will identify people, events, movements or ideas that may be unfamiliar to non-specialist readers and will improve understanding of the document's historical context.

To promote readability, we have modernized spelling in most instances and punctuation in some instances. Occasionally we have inserted italicized text, enclosed in brackets, to bridge gaps in syntax occurring due to illegibility or apparent errors in the source documents. With regard to capitalization, however, we have allowed usage to stand where it is internally consistent, even when varying from today's usage, since authors writing about the proper assignment of powers to the three branches of our federal government may signal their understanding of the authority belonging to each through capitalization.

In sum, our intent is that the documents and their supporting material provide reliable and unique access to the richness of the American story.

Eric Sands, Associate Professor of Government, Berry College, selected the documents and wrote the introductions, notes, and study questions. It was copyedited by Holly Halvorson Southern. Ali Brosky and David Tucker provided editorial support. This publication was made possible through the support of a grant by the John Templeton Foundation. The opinions expressed in this publication are those of the editors and do not necessarily reflect the views of the John Templeton Foundation.

Sarah A. Morgan Smith
Fellow

Introduction

Political parties have a long and often convoluted history in American politics. Parties were initially anathema to the Founders and the system laid
out in the Constitution was explicitly designed not to be reliant on political
parties. To the Founders, parties were factions that threatened to divide the
nation into competing groups that, at the worst, could turn to violence to
advance their interests (Document 1). The Founders also feared that parties
would disrupt the separation of powers. This would be especially true in the
case of unified government where loyalty to party might come to interfere
with the system of checks and balances. Finally, the Founders worried that
political parties might stand in the way of effective representation. Elected
officials with party affiliations might be tempted to only represent those of
their own political party and leave party opponents without a voice. Given
these concerns, it is little wonder that the Founders did not want parties
participating in American government.

Yet within ten years of ratification of the Constitution, political parties
were alive and well in American politics. Clearly this was not party politics as
it is now known, but there was a rough party system and partisanship was as
pronounced as it was divisive. This leads to an interesting conundrum—how
did the political system become partisan within such a short time after the
formation of a government designed to avoid reliance on political parties?
Probably the leading answer to this question is that parties were understood
as being inevitable. More precisely, republican government does not work
well without being buttressed by political parties. Parties have proven to
be instruments through which voters can make choices about the policy
direction of the country. Parties allow minorities to form coalitions to create
majority rule, even if that rule is not always harmonious or stable. Parties
help build support for officeholders and serve as conduits of communication
to the masses and vice versa. Parties serve as schools of democracy where
citizens learn to associate and become attached to governing institutions.
Finally, parties mobilize voters and encourage voter participation at all levels
of democratic politics.

Inevitable or not, the party system did not emerge all at once: it grew and
developed through several distinct political eras. The first of these was the

Federalist Era where, under the influence of Alexander Hamilton, the Federalists embarked on an ambitious set of projects to develop an industrial, commercial economy, strengthen the presidency and the courts, and set out broad terrain for the president to exercise vast powers in the realm of foreign affairs. These projects and others were soon opposed vigorously by Madison and Jefferson, with Jefferson eventually allowing himself to be placed as the head of the opposition party. Madison and Jefferson's growing partisanship was easy for all to see (Documents 2, 3, 4). To be sure, these were not the highly organized political parties of the later nineteenth century but tended to be united behind strong individuals and maintained a more informal organizational structure. The parties did make use of the press, but it was still in its infancy and only a few party newspapers published party writings and attacks on opponents.

This new party, ultimately called the Democratic-Republican Party, saw victory in the election of 1800, thus marking the beginning of the second party era. Under Jeffersonian and then Madisonian rule, the Federalists began to wither and die as an opposition party and the country was left under one-party rule. But without an opposition to unite them, the Jeffersonians soon found themselves internally divided on issues ranging from war to internal improvements. This led to a fissure in 1824 with several different candidates contending for the presidency. This led some individuals, such as Martin Van Buren, to begin to argue for a wholesale reorganization of the party system (Documents 8, 9).

The late 1820s began the third era of party development, the establishment of permanent two-party competition in America. Martin Van Buren played a major role in making this change possible. For Van Buren, the American electoral system was plagued with several major flaws that needed correcting. It was prone to factionalism with several candidates trying to win over different parts of the country to make the runoff election in the House. It encouraged perpetual campaigning with nothing to formally begin and end the campaign process. It fostered demagoguery with nothing to moderate the messages from the candidates. And it suffered from lack of legitimacy with elections to be decided by the House of Representatives instead of the Electoral College.[1] Van Buren's solution to all these problems was permanent two-party competition for America, and he began carrying out his vision

---

[1] James Ceaser, *Presidential Selection* (Princeton: Princeton University Press, 1979), 131–149.

by recruiting Andrew Jackson to form a new political party to compete in American politics (Documents 8, 9). Thus was born the Democratic Party which has been a fixture in American politics ever since.

A few years later, the second part of Van Buren's equation came into being with the birth of the Whig Party. Steadily increasing rates of voter turnout were one sign of the influence that the parties were having on American politics. This is not to say that voting was always well informed, but it was carried out by millions of Americans each election cycle. The parties at this time also developed the convention system for nominating candidates to office. Starting at the local level, conventions would meet to nominate delegates to the next convention level going all the way up to the national conventions. These conventions were highly participatory and helped reflect voter choices in the selection of national candidates.

The fourth era of American party development came with the demise of the Whig Party. The Whigs largely defined themselves as being opposed to Andrew Jackson. Once Jackson left office, the Whigs were left with a void in their policy stances. They did support internal improvements and tended to take hard stands on moral issues. The one moral issue they refused to address, however, was slavery. The Whigs joined in the various compromises on slavery that the parties negotiated to keep the sections at peace with one another, but they did not take a hard stand on the immorality of slavery or oppose its spread into the territories. As the abolitionist movement grew in scale and influence, pressure mounted on the Whigs to take a position. When they failed to do so, a new political party was formed that eventually replaced the Whigs—the Republicans. The election of the first Republican president, Abraham Lincoln, precipitated the Civil War, and Lincoln's victory in that war gave Republicans ascendency in American politics for a long time to come (Documents 12, 13, 14). At the same time, the two parties that would define American politics for the future were now firmly in place and Van Buren's vision of permanent two-party competition seemed to have come to fruition.

By the end of Reconstruction, the parties were once again on equal footing and they began trading election victories and control over the patronage, also known as the spoils of victory. For the winning party, this meant installing party loyalists into positions in the bureaucracy, exchanging jobs for vote support. This period of time represents the apex of party control and influence over the electorate. For some, participation in a political party took on an almost religious dimension, providing a sense of identity as well as purpose as they worked to further the party's political agenda. This is the era when bosses, politically influential individuals who control votes and appointments, emerged to run the big city machines that featured widespread corruption but also provided useful social services to their constituents (Document 20). These machines were party organizations, usually headed by a boss, that secured enough votes to maintain control of a city, county, or state.

Voter turnout was never as high as it was during this post-Reconstruction Era, and parties did a superlative job mobilizing voters and getting their people to the polls. Corruption at the polls certainly took place, but it tended to be particularized to certain areas and was definitely not all encompassing given the sheer number of voters participating. This period might truly be called the Golden Age of parties, which were considered a natural and organic part of the political system. Third parties also continued to emerge during this era including the Prohibition Party, the Greenback Party and the Populist Party (Document 17), though all were overshadowed by the dominance of the two-party system. This shows that there were undercurrents of discontent among the American electorate, but for the time being the two major parties were able to manage it.

In the 1890s, the course of American party eras becomes a bit murky. It becomes difficult to define what constitutes an era and what marks the beginning and ending of eras in the permanent two-party landscape. For instance, someone could argue that the election of 1896 marks the beginning of an era of Republican dominance following McKinley's triumph over William Jennings Bryan and the combined forces of the Democratic Party and the Populists (Document 18). Republicans would control both houses of Congress and the presidency until the election of 1912. That being said, the gaps between the parties in Congress were quite narrow at times and the Democrats maintained enough support to influence congressional politics. Thus the characterization of this era remains somewhat uncertain.

The Progressive Era marks another period for which an argument can be made that party development did occur. The Progressives alternately tried to destroy or reform political parties and brought about major changes to party politics in the process (Document 21):

- the introduction of civil service reform that weakened party control over patronage (the practice of awarding government jobs for political loyalty);

- the Australian ballot (also known as the secret ballot that allowed voters to select candidates without the parties knowing who they were voting for), which lessened party influence at the ballot box;
- the advent of primaries (having nominees elected by voters rather than chosen by convention), which diminished party control over the nomination process; and
- proposals for the implementation of more direct types of voter participation in the democratic process through initiatives (allowing citizens to bypass their state legislatures placing proposed statutes on the ballot), referendums (a general vote by the electorate on a political question that has been referred to them), and recalls (a vote to remove an elected representative from office before the end of his or her term) (Documents 22, 23, 24).

All these do not even take into account the constitutional amendments creating the direct election of senators and giving women the right to vote, both of which further altered the party system by giving the people direct control over senators and having women double the size of the electorate, forcing the party system to reorganize to take into account this massive influx of new voters.

Another political era agreed on by many party scholars is the election of 1932 and the rise of Franklin Roosevelt. Roosevelt's willingness to take on the role of party leader gave him powerful influence in Congress and allowed him to advance a programmatic agenda for the nation. The new Democratic coalition would prove a stable force for Roosevelt to build his programs and carry them into practice. That being said, Roosevelt's efforts at building a modern state and centering national leadership in the presidency had the effect of displacing parties as agents of popular rule (Documents 27, 28). In short, the New Deal state took over for many party responsibilities and weakened political parties as a consequence. Combined with the Progressive reforms of the earlier era, parties exited the New Deal Era considerably weaker, mere shadows of their former selves.

A final era that could be defined in party development is Ronald Reagan's election in 1980. Reagan, in this view, represents the culmination of conservative social movement politics that had its origins as far back as the 1960s (Document 31). A programmatic Republican Party was replaced with the politics of ideology, and Reagan was able to sell conservatism to the American public with his charisma and optimism (Document 34). Since that time the

Republicans have been a party of ideology that puts loyalty to ideas ahead of compromise and conciliation. Moreover, there is some evidence that the Democratic Party has followed suit and become more ideological as well. Whether party politics are well served from being influenced by ideology is still being worked out in American politics today.

What is clear is that political parties in the twenty-first century bear a scant resemblance to their predecessors in the eighteenth, nineteenth, or twentieth centuries, and the chances of returning to an earlier era of party governance seems remote. Yet contemporary problems like voter alienation, low voter participation rates, government gridlock, and low popular trust in government may all have their roots in the weakening of political parties. Parties have traditionally been laboratories where people develop the habits of associating with others, the techniques of accommodation, and attachment to government institutions. What parties need is a sense of public purpose, but it is unlikely that this purpose is going to come from the parties themselves. Instead, the parties need strong leadership that can infuse public purpose into the parties and lead them to restored prominence and relevance in American politics. American parties are far from perfect, but they may be needed now more than ever to restore American politics from the twin dangers of cynicism and indifference. Given the traditional roles of parties, we must think seriously about whether a rejuvenation of the parties might be an elixir for our contemporary ills.

Political Parties

CORE DOCUMENTS

Federalist 10

Publius (James Madison)

November 22, 1787

*F*ederalist 10 *was written by James Madison and is probably the most famous of the eighty-five papers written in support of ratification of the Constitution that are collectively known as the Federalist Papers. The Federalist essays were formally addressed to the people of New York and were intended to influence the New York ratifying convention. Other essays had been written that defended the Constitution primarily by attacking those who opposed it. What made the Federalist unique was that it defended the proposed Constitution by explaining in careful detail its provisions and the principles behind them.*

Though Alexander Hamilton, John Jay, and James Madison collaborated on the essays that make up the Federalist, *the three men wrote collectively under the pseudonym "Publius," indicating their intention to speak in a single voice through the essays. Federalist 10 specifically deals with Publius' treatment of factions and how a republican government can be constructed to protect against this dangerous malady. Factions, to Publius, were considered the bane of republican government, especially when a faction became a majority within the population. Factions were groups of people united by a common interest or passion adverse to the rights of other people in society. This oppressive nature of factions is what made them so dangerous and why Publius devoted so much time to discussing how to check and control them. In addition, Publius understood political parties to be factions and, in fact, uses "party" as a synonym for "faction" throughout* Federalist 10.

SOURCE: *The Federalist.* Gideon Edition, eds. George W. Carey and James McClellan (Indianapolis: Liberty Fund, 2001), 42–49.

... By a faction, I understand a number of citizens, whether amounting to a majority or minority of the whole, who are united and actuated by some common impulse of passion, or of interest, adverse to the rights of other citizens, or to the permanent and aggregate interests of the community.

There are two methods of curing the mischiefs of faction: The one, by removing its causes; the other, by controlling its effects.

There are again two methods of removing the causes of faction: The one, by destroying the liberty which is essential to its existence; the other, by giving to every citizen the same opinions, the same passions, and the same interests.

It could never be more truly said, than of the first remedy, that it is worse than the disease. Liberty is to faction, what air is to fire, an aliment,[1] without which it instantly expires. But it could not be a less folly to abolish liberty, which is essential to political life, because it nourishes faction, than it would be to wish the annihilation of air, which is essential to animal life, because it imparts to fire its destructive agency.

The second expedient is as impracticable, as the first would be unwise. As long as the reason of man continues fallible, and he is at liberty to exercise it, different opinions will be formed. As long as the connection subsists between his reason and his self-love, his opinions and his passions will have a reciprocal influence on each other; and the former will be objects to which the latter will attach themselves. The diversity in the faculties of men, from which the rights of property originate, is not less an insuperable obstacle to a uniformity of interests. The protection of these faculties, is the first object of government. From the protection of different and unequal faculties of acquiring property, the possession of different degrees and kinds of property immediately results; and from the influence of these on the sentiments and views of the respective proprietors, ensues a division of the society into different interests and parties.

The latent causes of faction are thus sown in the nature of man; and we see them every where brought into different degrees of activity, according to the different circumstances of civil society. A zeal for different opinions concerning religion, concerning government, and many other points, as well of speculation as of practice; an attachment to different leaders, ambitiously contending for pre-eminence and power; or to persons of other descriptions, whose fortunes have been interesting to the human passions, have, in turn, divided mankind into parties, inflamed them with mutual animosity, and rendered them much more disposed to vex and oppress each other, than to co-operate for their common good. So strong is this propensity of mankind, to fall into mutual animosities, that where no substantial occasion presents itself, the most frivolous and fanciful distinctions have been sufficient to

---

[1] element

kindle their unfriendly passions, and excite their most violent conflicts. But the most common and durable source of factions, has been the various and unequal distribution of property. Those who hold, and those who are without property, have ever formed distinct interests in society. Those who are creditors, and those who are debtors, fall under a like discrimination. A landed interest, a manufacturing interest, a mercantile interest, a monied interest, with many lesser interests, grow up of necessity in civilized nations, and divide them into different classes, actuated by different sentiments and views. The regulation of these various and interfering interests, forms the principal task of modern legislation, and involves the spirit of party and faction in the necessary and ordinary operations of government....

It is in vain to say, that enlightened statesmen will be able to adjust these clashing interests, and render them all subservient to the public good. Enlightened statesmen will not always be at the helm: nor, in many cases, can such an adjustment be made at all, without taking into view indirect and remote considerations, which will rarely prevail over the immediate interest which one party may find in disregarding the right of another, or the good of the whole.

The inference to which we are brought, is, that the *causes* of faction cannot be removed; and that relief is only to be sought in the means of controlling its *effects*.

If a faction consists of less than a majority, relief is supplied by the republican principle, which enables the majority to defeat its sinister views, by regular vote. It may clog the administration, it may convulse the society; but it will be unable to execute and mask its violence under the forms of the constitution. When a majority is included in a faction, the form of popular government, on the other hand, enables it to sacrifice to its ruling passion or interest, both the public good and the rights of other citizens. To secure the public good, and private rights, against the danger of such a faction, and at the same time to preserve the spirit and the form of popular government, is then the great object to which our inquiries are directed. Let me add, that it is the great desideratum,[2] by which alone this form of government can be rescued from the opprobrium under which it has so long labored, and be recommended to the esteem and adoption of mankind.

By what means is this object attainable? Evidently by one of two only. Either the existence of the same passion or interest in a majority, at the same time, must be prevented; or the majority, having such co-existent passion or

---

[2] A thing needed or desired.

interest, must be rendered, by their number and local situation, unable to concert[3] and carry into effect schemes of oppression. If the impulse and the opportunity be suffered to coincide, we well know, that neither moral nor religious motives can be relied on as an adequate control. They are not found to be such on the injustice and violence of individuals, and lose their efficacy in proportion to the number combined together; that is, in proportion as their efficacy becomes needful.

From this view of the subject, it may be concluded, that a pure democracy, by which I mean, a society consisting of a small number of citizens, who assemble and administer the government in person, can admit of no cure for the mischiefs of faction. A common passion or interest will, in almost every case, be felt by a majority of the whole; a communication and concert, results from the form of government itself; and there is nothing to check the inducements to sacrifice the weaker party, or an obnoxious individual. Hence it is, that such democracies have ever been spectacles of turbulence and contention; have ever been found incompatible with personal security, or the rights of property; and have, in general, been as short in their lives, as they have been violent in their deaths. Theoretic politicians, who have patronized this species of government, have erroneously supposed, that, by reducing mankind to a perfect equality in their political rights, they would, at the same time, be perfectly equalized and assimilated in their possessions, their opinions, and their passions.

A republic, by which I mean a government in which the scheme of representation takes place, opens a different prospect, and promises the cure for which we are seeking. Let us examine the points in which it varies from pure democracy, and we shall comprehend both the nature of the cure and the efficacy which it must derive from the union.

The two great points of difference, between a democracy and a republic, are, first, the delegation of the government, in the latter, to a small number of citizens elected by the rest; secondly, the greater number of citizens, and greater sphere of country, over which the latter may be extended.

The effect of the first difference is, on the one hand, to refine and enlarge the public views, by passing them through the medium of a chosen body of citizens, whose wisdom may best discern the true interest of their country, and whose patriotism and love of justice, will be least likely to sacrifice it to temporary or partial considerations. Under such a regulation, it may well happen, that the public voice, pronounced by the representatives of the

---

[3] To coordinate or organize.

people, will be more consonant to the public good, than if pronounced by the
people themselves, convened for the purpose. On the other hand, the effect
may be inverted. Men of factious tempers, of local prejudices, or of sinister
designs, may by intrigue, by corruption, or by other means, first obtain the
suffrages, and then betray the interests of the people.…

The other point of difference is, the great number of citizens, and extent
of territory, which may be brought within the compass of republican, than
of democratic government; and it is this circumstance principally which
renders factious combinations less to be dreaded in the former, than in the
latter. The smaller the society, the fewer probably will be the distinct parties
and interests composing it; the fewer the distinct parties and interests, the
more frequently will a majority be found of the same party; and the smaller
the number of individuals composing a majority, and the smaller the compass
within which they are placed, the more easily will they concert and execute
their plans of oppression. Extend the sphere, and you take in a greater variety of parties and interests; you make it less probable that a majority of the
whole will have a common motive to invade the rights of other citizens; or
if such a common motive exists, it will be more difficult for all who feel it to
discover their own strength, and to act in unison with each other. Besides
other impediments, it may be remarked, that where there is a consciousness
of unjust or dishonorable purposes, communication is always checked by
distrust, in proportion to the number whose concurrence is necessary.…

The influence of factious leaders may kindle a flame within their particular states, but will be unable to spread a general conflagration through the
other states; a religious sect may degenerate into a political faction in a part
of the confederacy; but the variety of sects dispersed over the entire face of
it, must secure the national councils against any danger from that source: a
rage for paper money, for an abolition of debts, for an equal division of property, or for any other improper or wicked project, will be less apt to pervade
the whole body of the union, than a particular member of it; in the same
proportion as such a malady is more likely to taint a particular county or
district, than an entire state.…

"Parties"

James Madison

January 23, 1792

T*he American nation was only a few years old before parties began to form and partisan disagreement emerged as open hostility. On one side were the Federalists who were formed chiefly by Alexander Hamilton during his tenure in Washington's cabinet. The Federalist Party believed in a strong central government and tended to favor the less democratic institutions of government such as the presidency and the judiciary. The Federalists also advocated a national banking system and attempted to establish good trade relations with England. Opposed to these views were the Democratic-Republicans who would eventually fall under the leadership of Thomas Jefferson. The Jeffersonians favored an agricultural economic base rather than one based on banking, opposed the idea of strengthening ties with Great Britain and favored the rule of the people and the more democratic part of American government—the Legislature.*

In the growing confrontation with the Hamiltonian Federalists, Madison agreed to write a series of essays for the National Gazette on political economy and fundamental republican principles. Several of those essays came to focus on political parties. The first, "Parties," argued that a republican government should help to ensure political equality, create an equitable distribution of property and refuse to grant special privileges. These measures would help to alleviate unnecessary partisan strife. Parties should be based on natural differences among the people rather than the artificial differences favored by the Hamiltonians. This would include differences of merit or talent versus differences based on property or wealth.

SOURCE: "For the National Gazette, [ca. 23 January] 1792," Founders Online, National Archives, https://founders.archives.gov/documents/Madison/01-14-02-0176.

[Editor's note: We have changed the formatting of Madison's enumeration of the objections to parties; in the original, the list appears as running text in the body of his first paragraph, but for the sake of readability, we present it here as a numbered list.]

IN every political society, parties are unavoidable. A difference of interests, real or supposed is the most natural and fruitful source of them. The great object should be to combat the evil:

1. By establishing a political equality among all.
2. By withholding unnecessary opportunities from a few, to increase the inequality of property, by an immoderate, and especially an unmerited, accumulation of riches.
3. By the silent operation of laws, which, without violating the rights of property, reduce extreme wealth towards a slate of mediocrity, and raise extreme indigence towards a slate of comfort.
4. By abstaining from measures which operate differently on different interests, and particularly such as favor one interest at the expense of another.
5. By making one party a check on the other, so far as the existence of parties cannot be prevented, nor their views accommodated.—If this is not the language of reason, it is that of republicanism.

In all political societies, different interests and parties arise out of the nature of things, and the great art of politicians lies in making them checks and balances to each other. Let us then increase these *natural distinctions* by favoring an inequality of property; and let us add to them *artificial di[st] inctions,* by establishing *kings,* and *nobles,* and *plebeians.* We shall then have the more checks to oppose to each other; we shall then have the more scales and the more weights to perfect and maintain the equilibrium. This is as little the voice of reason, as it is that of republicanism.

From the expediency, in politics, of making natural parties, mutual checks on each other, to infer the propriety of creating artificial parties, in order to form them into mutual checks, is not less absurd than it would be in ethics, to say, that new vices ought to be promoted, where they would counteract each other, because this use may be made of existing vices.

"A Candid State of Parties"

James Madison

September 22, 1792

"A Candid State of Parties" is another essay written by Madison for the National Gazette. Here, Madison writes from what seems to be a clearly partisan point of view, declaring that the Federalists, "from natural temper, or from habits of life, are more partial to the opulent than to the other classes of society; and having debauched themselves into a persuasion that mankind are incapable of governing themselves, it follows with them, of course, that government can be carried on only by the pageantry of rank, the influence of money and emoluments, and the terror of military force." A government of private interest in the place of public duty that depended upon bribes, privileges and selfishness was a false government. Clearly, Madison had in mind the British government and warned that Hamilton and the Federalists were taking the country in that direction.

Having accused the Federalists of preferring the interests of the few to the many and of failing to trust in the ruling wisdom of the people, Madison finds his way clear to applaud his own Democratic-Republican Party. In contrast to the perfidy of the Federalists, Madison frames the Democratic-Republican Party as a friend to the people and the true guardian of republican government. The alternative was regression into monarchy and a return to the type of British rule that the Americans had so valiantly cast off.

SOURCE: "For the National Gazette, 22 September 1792," Founders Online, National Archives, accessed April 11, 2019, https://founders.archives.gov/documents/Madison/01-14-02-0334.

As it is the business of the contemplative statesman to trace the history of parties in a free country, so it is the duty of the citizen at all times to understand the actual state of them. Whenever this duty is omitted, an opportunity is given to designing men, by the use of artificial or nominal distinctions, to oppose and balance against each other those who never differed as to the end to be pursued, and may no longer differ as to the means of attaining it. The most interesting state of parties in the United States may be referred to three periods: Those who espoused the cause of independence and those who adhered to the British claims, formed the parties of the first period; if, indeed, the disaffected class were considerable enough to deserve the name of a party. This state of things was superseded by the treaty of peace in 1783. From 1783 to 1787 there were parties in abundance, but being rather local than general, they are not within the present review.

The Federal Constitution, proposed in the latter year, gave birth to a second and most interesting division of the people. Every one remembers it, because every one was involved in it.

Among those who embraced the constitution, the great body were unquestionably friends to republican liberty; tho' there were, no doubt, some who were openly or secretly attached to monarchy and aristocracy; and hoped to make the constitution a cradle for these hereditary establishments.

Among those who opposed the constitution, the great body were certainly well affected to the union and to good government, tho' there might be a few who had a leaning unfavorable to both. This state of parties was terminated by the regular and effectual establishment of the federal government in 1788; out of the administration of which, however, has arisen a third division, which being natural to most political studies, is likely to be of some duration in ours.

One of the divisions consists of those, who from particular interest, from natural temper, or from the habits of life, are more partial to the opulent than to the other classes of society; and having debauched themselves into a persuasion that mankind are incapable of governing themselves, it follows with them, of course, that a government can be carried on only by the pageantry of rank, the influence of money and emoluments, and the terror of military force. Men of those sentiments must naturally wish to point the measures of government less to the interest of the many than of a few, and less to the reason of the many than to their weaknesses; hoping perhaps in proportion to the ardor of their zeal, that by giving such a turn to the administration, the government itself may by degrees be narrowed into fewer hands, and approximated to an hereditary form.

The other division consists of those who believing in the doctrine that mankind are [sic] capable of governing themselves, and hating hereditary power as an insult to the reason and an outrage to the rights of man, are naturally offended at every public measure that does not appeal to the understanding and to the general interest of the community, or that is not strictly conformable to the principles, and conducive to the preservation of republican government.

This being the real state of parties among us, an experienced and dispassionate observer will be at no loss to decide on the probable conduct of each.

The antirepublican party, as it may be called, being the weaker in point of numbers, will be induced by the most obvious motives to strengthen themselves with the men of influence, particularly of moneyed, which is the most active and insinuating influence. It will be equally their true policy to weaken their opponents by reviving exploded parties, and taking advantage of all prejudices, local, political, and occupational, that may prevent or disturb a general coalition of sentiments.

The Republican party, as it may be termed, conscious that the mass of people in every part of the union, in every state, and of every occupation must at bottom be with them, both in interest and sentiment, will naturally find their account in burying all antecedent questions, in banishing every other distinction than that between enemies and friends to republican government, and in promoting a general harmony among the latter, wherever residing, or however employed.

Whether the republican or the rival party will ultimately establish its ascendance, is a problem which may be contemplated now; but which time alone can solve. On one hand experience shews that in politics as in war, stratagem is often an overmatch for numbers: and among more happy characteristics of our political situation, it is now well understood that there are peculiarities, some temporary, others more durable,[1] which may favor that side in the contest. On the republican side, again, the superiority of numbers is so great, their sentiments are so decided, and the practice of making a common cause, where there is a common sentiment and common interest, in spite of circumstantial and artificial distinctions, is so well understood, that no temperate observer of human affairs will be surprised if the issue in the present instance should be reversed, and the government be administered in the spirit and form approved by the great body of the people.

---

[1] Madison believed that Washington's association with the Federalist Party gave it an artificial boost in public opinion, but that Washington's influence could not last forever and when his time past the people would return to their natural home in the Republican Party.

Letter to Philip Mazzei

Thomas Jefferson

April 24, 1796

A merican expatriate Philip Mazzei (1730–1816) was Jefferson's former neighbor and was living in Pisa at the time the letter was written. Mazzei's motivation for revealing the content of the letter remains unclear, but the reason might
have been simple carelessness or a lack of awareness that the letter could adversely
affect Jefferson. The contents of the letter were intended to be confidential but
Mazzei made several copies of relevant parts of the letter and sent them to friends.
The letter was then published in a French newspaper along with an editorial that
was highly critical of U.S. foreign policy. Several months later, Noah Webster, the
Federalist editor of the New York Minerva, had the letter translated into English
and then printed it in his newspaper. The letter proved highly embarrassing for
Jefferson and encouraged Federalist criticisms that Jefferson and his emerging
party were more loyal to France than to America. Jefferson was even accused
of treason and the letter was interpreted as a vailed personal attack on George
Washington. The incident taught Jefferson to use much greater caution in his
personal correspondence but the letter continued to haunt Jefferson for the rest
of his political career.

SOURCE: "I. Thomas Jefferson to Philip Mazzei, 24 April 1796," Founders Online,
National Archives, accessed April 11, 2019, https://founders.archives.gov/documents/
Jefferson/01-29-02-0054-0002.

My dear friend,
Monticello Apr. 24. 1796.
    … The aspect of our politics has wonderfully changed since you left us. In
place of that noble love of liberty, and republican government which carried
us triumphantly thro' the war, an Anglican, monarchical and aristocratical
party has sprung up, whose avowed object is to draw over us the substance as
they have already done the forms of the British government. The main body
of our citizens however remain true to their republican principles, the whole

landed interest is with them (republican), and so is a great mass of talents. Against us are the Executive, the Judiciary, two out of three branches of the legislature, all the officers of the government, all who want to be officers, all timid men who prefer the calm of despotism to the boisterous sea of liberty, British merchants and Americans trading on British capitals, speculators and holders in the banks and public funds a contrivance invented for the purposes of corruption and for assimilating us in all things, to the rotten as well as the sound parts of the British model. It would give you a fever were I to name to you the apostates who have gone over to these heresies, men who were Samsons in the field and Solomons in the council, but who have had their heads shorn by the harlot England.[1] In short we are likely to preserve the liberty we have obtained only be unremitting labors and perils. But we shall preserve them [sic], and our mass of weight and wealth on the good side is so great as to leave no danger that force will ever be attempted against us. We have only to awake and snap the Lilliputian cords with which they have been entangling us during the first sleep which succeeded our labors....[2]

> Your friend and servant
> TH: JEFFERSON

---

[1] Here Jefferson alludes to two Biblical figures: Samson, a judge and military leader renowned for his superhuman strength, and Solomon, regarded as Israel's wisest king. Both men were also famously susceptible to the wiles of beautiful women, and Samson (whose strength was symbolically linked to his vow as a Nazarene not to cut his hair) enabled both his own capture and the defeat of his people when he allowed the prostitute Delilah to cut his hair. This line was generally understood as an attack on outgoing president George Washington.

[2] An allusion to the satirical novel *Gulliver's Travels*, by Jonathan Swift, in which the title character awakes to find himself bound on the shore of a far distant land after a shipwreck. In this land, known as Lilliput, Gulliver (an ordinary Englishman) is a giant; he easily snaps his captors' diminutive ropes and regains his freedom.

Letter to Thomas Jefferson

President George Washington

July 6, 1796

*D*uring the furor over Jefferson's letter to Mazzei (Document 4) and the partisan rancor it caused, Washington remained publicly silent, even though many Federalists construed the letter as an attack on Washington himself. Prior to the letter's publication, Washington sent a letter to Jefferson commenting on the display of partisan politics in the country and also offering advice and suggestions on farming techniques. Washington's correspondence displays his magnanimous nature and his desire to remain above what he considered petty partisan politics. To be sure, however, the Mazzei letter strained the relationship between Jefferson and Washington.*

Jefferson had served as secretary of state under Washington but often found himself at odds with Secretary of the Treasury Alexander Hamilton, who seemed to have the president's ear. In 1793 Jefferson resigned as secretary of state and returned to Virginia where he worked to spread the influence of the new Democratic-Republican Party he had helped to found. He returned to national politics in 1796 as vice president under John Adams, with whom he often had a difficult relationship. The publication of the Mazzei letter did not help things and the Federalist press attacked Jefferson mercilessly. Washington, however, made no public comments about the letter, nor did he ever rebuke Jefferson privately. Jefferson, meanwhile, used the Republican press to fight back over the letter and to prepare for his run at the presidency in 1800.

SOURCE: George Washington to Thomas Jefferson, July 6, 1796, George Washington Papers, Series 2, Letterbooks 1754–1799, Library of Congress. http://cdn.loc.gov/service/mss/mgw/mgw2/019/019.pdf.

Dear Sir,

When I inform you that your letter of the 19th ultimo went to Philadelphia and returned to this place [Mount Vernon], before it was received by me, it

will be admitted, I am persuaded, as an apology for my not having acknowledged the receipt of it sooner.

If I had entertained any suspicions before, that the queries which have
been published in Bache's paper proceeded from you, the assurances you
have given of the contrary, would have removed them; but the truth is, I
harbored none. I am at no loss to *conjecture* from what source they flowed;
through what channel they were conveyed; and for what purpose they, and
similar publications, appear. They were known to be in the hands of Mr.
Parker[1] in the early part of the last Session of Congress. They were shown
about by Mr. Giles[2] during the Session and they made their public exhibition
about the close of it.

Perceiving, and probably hearing, that no abuse in the gazettes would
induce me to take notice of anonymous publications against me, those who
were disposed to do me *such friendly offices*, have embraced without restraint,
every opportunity to weaken the confidence of the People; and by having the
whole game in their hands, they have scrupled not to publish things that do
not, as well as those which do exist; and to mutilate the latter, so as to make
them subserve the purposes which they have in view.

As you have mentioned the subject yourself, it would not be frank, candid
or friendly to conceal that your conduct has been represented as derogatory[3]
from that opinion I had conceived you entertained of me. That to your particular friends and connections, you have described, and they have denounced
me as a person under a dangerous influence; and that if I would listen *more*
to some *other* opinions, all would be well. My answer invariably has been
that I had never discovered anything in the conduct of Mr. Jefferson to raise
suspicions in my mind, of his insincerity; that if he would retrace my public
conduct while he was in the Administration, abundant proofs would occur
to him, that truth and right decisions were the *sole* objects of my pursuit;
that there were as many instances within his *own* knowledge of my having
decided *against* as in *favor* of the opinions of the person evidently alluded
to;[4] and moreover that I was no believer in the infallibility of the politics or

---

[1] Josiah Parker (1751–1810), Federalist, Representative from Virginia.
[2] William Branch Giles (1762–1830), Democratic-Republican, Representative from
Virginia.
[3] In the original text; perhaps Washington intended to write "derogating."
[4] Alexander Hamilton (1755 or 1757–1804), Jefferson's nemesis in the administration
due to his support of England as a commercial partner for the United States.

measures of *any man living*. In short that I was no party man myself, and the first wish of my heart was, if parties did exist, to reconcile them.

To this I may add, and very truly, that until within the last year or two I had no conception that parties would, or even could go the length I have been witness to; nor did I believe, until lately, that it was within the bounds of probability; hardly within those of possibility, that while I was using my utmost exertions to establish a national character of our own; independent, as far as our obligations and justice would permit of every nation of the earth; and wished by steering a steady course to preserve this country from the honors of a desolating war, that I should be accused of being the enemy of one nation, and subject to the influence of another;[5] and to prove it that every act of my administration would be tortured, and the grossest and most insidious misrepresentations of them be made, (by giving one side *only* of a subject, and that too in such exaggerated and indecent terms, as could scarcely be applied to a Negro; a notorious defaulter; or even to a common pick-pocket).[6] But enough of this. I have already gone farther in the expression of my feelings, than I intended . . . [source document ends with ellipses]

---

[5] While Washington favored a foreign policy of neutrality in the conflict between France and England on the grounds that the nation was too immature to engage in another military engagement, he was accused by Republicans of reneging on the nation's treaty with France and of falling prey to the wiles of the British.

[6] Here, Washington suggests that the accusations leveled against him are so outrageous they would be offensive even to those with no reputations to lose, referring to African-Americans, debtors, and even thieves.

Farewell Address

President George Washington

September 19, 1796

I t is likely that Article II of the Constitution would not have been written as it
was were it not for the knowledge that George Washington would serve as the
*first president, and indeed, he was unanimously elected to office. Washington not
only proved to be a capable chief executive but to be conscientious in the way he
established many of the unspecified precedents and protocols surrounding the
office. Yet Washington quickly tired of public life and intended to retire after his
first term. He asked James Madison to help him prepare a retirement address to
the American people that would articulate his vision for how the United States
could become a flourishing and prosperous nation. Washington's friends, however, convinced him to serve a second term of office despite his reluctance. As his
second term neared completion, Washington again stated his intention to retire,
this time asking Alexander Hamilton to revise Madison's earlier draft into what
would become his Farewell Address. The address puts on display Washington's
fear of political parties, a concern shared by many of his contemporaries.*

*A further point of interest is that the Senate engages in an annual reading of
President Washington's Farewell Address by a current member of the U.S. Senate. The tradition started in 1862 and became an annual event in 1893. After the
appointed senator reads the address in legislative session, he or she signs his or
her name in Washington's Farewell Address Book.*

SOURCE: Farewell Address, George Washington, September 19, 1796. Online by Gerhard
Peters and John T. Wolley, *The American Presidency Project*. https://www.presidency.ucsb.
edu/node/200675.

To the People of the United States.

Friends and Fellow-Citizens,

The period for a new election of a Citizen, to administer the executive
government of the United States, being not far distant, and the time actually
arrived, when your thoughts must be employed in designating the person,

who is to be clothed with that important trust, it appears to me proper, especially as it may conduce to a more distinct expression of the public voice, that I should now apprise you of the resolution I have formed, to decline being considered among the number of those, out of whom a choice is to be made.

I beg you, at the same time, to do me the justice to be assured, that this resolution has not been taken, without a strict regard to all the considerations appertaining to the relation, which binds a dutiful citizen to his Country; and that, in with drawing the tender of service which silence in my situation might imply, I am influenced by no diminution of zeal for your future interest; no deficiency of grateful respect for your past kindness; but am supported by a full conviction that the step is compatible with both....

...I rejoice, that the state of your concerns, external as well as internal, no longer renders the pursuit of inclination incompatible with the sentiment of duty, or propriety; and am persuaded whatever partiality may be retained for my services, that in the present circumstances of our Country, you will not disapprove my determination to retire...

...Here, perhaps, I ought to stop. But a solicitude for your own welfare, which cannot end but with my life, and the apprehension of danger, natural to that solicitude, urge me on an occasion like the present, to offer to your solemn contemplation, and to recommend to your frequent review some sentiments, which are the result of much reflection, of no inconsiderable observation, and which appear to me all important to the permanency of your felicity as a people. These will be offered to you with the more freedom, as you can only see in them the disinterested warnings of a parting friend, who can possibly have no personal motive to bias his Council. Nor can I forget, as an encouragement to it, your indulgent reception of my sentiments on a former and not dissimilar occasion.

...In contemplating the causes which may disturb our Union, it occurs as matter of serious concern, that any ground should have been furnished for characterizing parties by *Geographical* discriminations—*Northern* and *Southern*—*Atlantic* and *Western*; whence designing men may endeavor to excite a belief that there is a real difference of local Interests and views. One of the expedients of party to acquire influence, within particular districts, is to misrepresent the opinions and aims of other districts. You cannot shield yourselves too much against the jealousies and heart burnings which spring from these misrepresentations: they tend to render alien to each other those who ought to be bound together by fraternal affection. The inhabitants of our western country have lately had a useful lesson on this head: they have seen, in the negociation by the Executive, and in the unanimous ratification by the Senate, of the Treaty with Spain, and in the universal satisfaction of that event throughout the united states, a decisive proof how unfounded were the suspicions propagated among them of a policy in the General Government and in the Atlantic States unfriendly to their interests in regard to the Mississippi: they have been witnesses to the formation of two treaties, that with great Britain and that with Spain, which secure to them every thing they could desire, in respect to our foreign relations, towards confirming their prosperity. Will it not be their wisdom to rely for the preservation of these advantages on the Union by which they were procured? Will they not henceforth be deaf to those advisers, if such there are who would sever them from their Brethren and connect them with aliens?

...All obstructions to the execution of the Laws, all combinations and associations, under whatever plausible character, with the real design to direct, control, counteract, or awe the regular deliberation and action of the constituted authorities, are destructive of this fundamental principle, and of fatal tendency. They serve to organize faction, to give it an artificial and extraordinary force to put in the place of the delegated will of the nation, the will of party, often a small but artful and enterprising minority of the community; and according to the alternate triumphs of different parties, to make the public administration the mirror of the ill conceived and incongruous projects of faction, rather than the organ of consistent and wholesome plans digested by common councils, and modified by mutual interests.

...I have already intimated to you, the danger of parties in the state, with particular reference to the founding them on geographical discriminations. Let me now take a more comprehensive view, and warn you in the most solemn manner against the baneful effects of the spirit of party, Generally.—

This spirit, unfortunately, is inseparable from our nature, having its root in the strongest passions of the human mind. It exists under different shapes in all governments more or less stifled, controlled, or repressed; but in those of the popular form, it is seen in its greatest rankness and is truly their worst enemy.

The alternate domination of one faction over another, sharpened by the spirit of revenge, natural to party dissention, which in different ages and countries has perpetrated the most horrid enormities, is itself a frightful despotism. But this leads at length to a more formal and permanent despotism. The disorders and miseries, which result, gradually incline the minds of men to seek security and repose in the absolute power of an individual: and sooner or later the chief of some prevailing faction, more able or more fortunate than his competitors, turns this disposition to the purposes of is own elevation, on the ruins of Public Liberty.

Without looking forward to an extremity of this kind (which nevertheless ought not to be entirely ought of sight) the common and continual mischiefs of the spirit of party are sufficient to make it the interest and duty of a wise People to discourage and restrain it.

It serves always to distract the public councils and enfeeble the Public Administration. It agitates the Community with ill founded jealousies and false alarms; kindles the animosity of one part against another, foments occasionally riot and insurrection. It opens the door to foreign influence and corruption, which finds a facilitated access to the government itself through the channels of party passions. Thus the policy and the will of one country are subjected to the policy and will of another.

There is an opinion that parties in free countries are useful checks upon the administration of the Government, and serve to keep alive the spirit of Liberty. This within certain limits is probably true; and in Governments of a monarchical cast, Patriotism may look with indulgence, if not with favor upon the spirit of party. But in those of the popular character, in Governments purely elective, it is a spirit not to be encouraged. From their natural tendency, it is certain there will always be enough of that spirit for every salutary purpose. And there being constant danger of excess, the effort ought to be, by force of public opinion, to mitigate and assuage it. A fire not to be quenched; it demands a uniform vigilance to prevent its bursting into a flame, lest, instead of warming it should consume.

It is important likewise, that the habits of thinking in a free country, should inspire caution. In those entrusted with its administration, to confine themselves within their respective constitutional spheres. Avoiding in the exercise of the powers of one department to encroach upon another. The spirit of encroachment tends to consolidate the powers of all the departments in one, and thus to create, whatever the form of Government, a real despotism. A just estimate of that love of power, and proneness to abuse it, which predominates in the human heart, is sufficient to satisfy us of the truth of this position. The necessity of reciprocal checks in the exercise of political power; by dividing and distributing it into different depositories, and constituting each the guardian of the public weal against invasions by the others, has been evinced by experiments ancient and modern: some of them in our country and under our own eyes. To preserve them must be as necessary as to institute them. If, in the opinion of the People, the distribution or modification of the constitutional powers be in any particular wrong, let it be corrected by an amendment in the way which the constitution designates. But let there be no change by usurpation; for tho' this, in one instance, may be the instrument of good, it is the customary weapon by which free Governments are destroyed. The precedent must always greatly overbalance in permanent evil any partial or transient benefit which the use can at any time yield. . . .

First Inaugural Address

President Thomas Jefferson

March 4, 1801

*T*he election of 1800 was highly contentious, pitting Democratic-Republicans supporting Thomas Jefferson against Federalists supporting the reelection of John Adams (see Document 5). When the electoral votes were counted, Jefferson and Aaron Burr, his presidential running mate, received the same number of votes. (When the Electoral College was created, no one had anticipated that political parties would exist to nominate candidates for both offices, so such an eventuality had not been foreseen.) Following the protocol laid out in the Constitution, the election was sent to the House of Representatives where votes were taken by state with each state getting one vote. Unfortunately for Jefferson, the Federalists still controlled the House and many initially cast their votes in favor of Burr in an attempt to deny Jefferson the presidency. In the end, however, enough Federalists supported Jefferson for him to be elected president.

Despite the contentious nature of the election, the events did not produce violence among the electorate and the election set a precedent for the peaceful transfer of power from one political party to another. Jefferson's followers also passed the Twelfth Amendment requiring separate electoral votes for president and vice president to ensure the events of 1800 would not be repeated.

SOURCE: Inaugural Address, Thomas Jefferson, March 4, 1801. Online by Gerhard Peters and John T. Wolley, *The American Presidency Project*. https://www.presidency.ucsb.edu/node/201948.

Called upon to undertake the duties of the first executive office of our country, I avail myself of the presence of that portion of my fellow-citizens which is here assembled, to express my grateful thanks for the favor with which they have been pleased to look toward me, to declare a sincere consciousness, that the task is above my talents, and that I approach it with those anxious and awful presentiments which the greatness of the charge and the weakness of my powers so justly inspire. A rising nation, spread over a wide and fruitful land, traversing all the seas with the rich productions of their industry, engaged in commerce with nations who feel power and forget right, advancing rapidly to destinies beyond the reach of mortal eye—when I contemplate these transcendent objects, and see the honor, the happiness, and the hopes of this beloved country, committed to the issue and the auspices of this day, I shrink from the contemplation, and humble myself before the magnitude of the undertaking. Utterly, indeed, should I despair, did not the presence of many whom I here see remind me, that, in the other high authorities, provided by our Constitution I shall find resources of wisdom, of virtue, and of zeal, on which to rely under all difficulties. To you, then, gentlemen, who are charged with the sovereign functions of legislation, and to those associated with you, I look with encouragement for that guidance and support which may enable us to steer with safety the vessel in which we are all embarked amidst the conflicting elements of a troubled world.

During the contest of opinion through which we have passed the animation of discussions and of exertions has sometimes worn an aspect which might impose on strangers unused to think freely, and to write what they think; but this being now decided by the voice of the nation, announced according to the rules of the Constitution, all will, of course, arrange themselves under the will of the law, and unite in common efforts for the common good. All, too, will bear in mind this sacred principle, that though the will of the majority is in all cases to prevail, that will to be rightful must be reasonable; that the minority possess their equal rights, which equal laws must protect, and to violate would be oppression. Let us, then, fellow-citizens, unite with one heart and one mind. Let us restore to social intercourse that harmony and affection without which liberty and even life itself are but dreary things. And let us reflect that, having banished from our land that religious intolerance, under which mankind so long bled and suffered, we have yet gained little if we countenance a political intolerance as despotic, as wicked, and capable of as bitter and bloody persecutions. During the throes and convulsions of the ancient world, during the agonizing spasms of infuriated man, seeking through blood and slaughter his long-lost liberty, it was not wonderful that the agitation of the billows should reach even this distant and peaceful shore; that this should be more felt and feared by some and less by others, and should divide opinions as to measures of safety. But every difference of opinion is not a difference of principle. We have called by different names brethren of the same principle. We are all Republicans,[1] we are all

---

[1] That is, Democratic-Republicans.

Federalists. If there be any among us who would wish to dissolve this Union or to change its republican form, let them stand undisturbed as monuments of the safety with which error of opinion may be tolerated where reason is left free to combat it. I know, indeed, that some honest men fear a republican government cannot be strong, that this Government is not strong enough; but would the honest patriot, in the full tide of successful experiment, abandon a government which has so far kept us free and firm on the theoretic and visionary fear that this Government, the world's best hope, may by possibility want energy to preserve itself? I trust not. I believe this, on the contrary, the strongest Government on earth. I believe it the only one where every man, at the call of the law, would fly to the standard of the law, and would meet invasions of the public order as his own personal concern. Sometimes it is said that man cannot be trusted with the government of himself. Can he, then, be trusted with the government of others? Or have we found angels in the form of kings to govern him? Let history answer this question.

Let us, then, with courage and confidence, pursue our own Federal and Republican principles, our attachment to union and representative government. Kindly separated by nature and a wide ocean from the exterminating havoc of one quarter of the globe; too high-minded to endure the degradations of the others; possessing a chosen country, with room enough for our descendants to the thousandth and thousandth generation; entertaining a due sense of our equal right to the use of our own faculties, to the acquisitions of our own industry, to honor and confidence from our fellow-citizens, resulting not from birth, but from our actions and their sense of them; enlightened by a benign religion, professed, indeed, and practiced in various forms, yet all of them inculcating honesty, truth, temperance, gratitude, and the love of man; acknowledging and adoring an overruling Providence, which by all its dispensations proves that it delights in the happiness of man here and his greater happiness hereafter[2]—with all these blessings, what more is necessary to make us a happy and a prosperous people? Still one thing more, fellow-citizens—a wise and frugal Government, which shall restrain men from injuring one another, shall leave them otherwise free to regulate their own pursuits of industry and improvement, and shall not take from the

---

[2] Jefferson's invocation of religion is ironic here given that his Federalist opponents had accused him of being "an atheist in religion, and a fanatic in politics." Jefferson was seen as a defamer of churches and a man possessing little to no religious principles. The Inaugural Address casts him in a very different light and Jefferson here uses religion as a way of trying to reunite a fractured nation.

mouth of labor the bread it has earned. This is the sum of good government, and this is necessary to close the circle of our felicities.

About to enter, fellow-citizens, on the exercise of duties which comprehend everything dear and valuable to you, it is proper you should understand what I deem the essential principles of our Government, and consequently those which ought to shape its Administration. I will compress them within the narrowest compass they will bear, stating the general principle, but not all its limitations. Equal and exact justice to all men, of whatever state or persuasion, religious or political; peace, commerce, and honest friendship with all nations, entangling alliances with none; the support of the State governments in all their rights, as the most competent administrations for our domestic concerns and the surest bulwarks against anti-republican tendencies; the preservation of the General Government in its whole constitutional vigor, as the sheet anchor of our peace at home, and safety abroad; a zealous care of the right of election by the people—a mild and safe corrective of abuses which are lopped by the sword of revolution where peaceable remedies are unprovided; absolute acquiescence in the decisions of the majority, the vital principle of republics, from which there is no appeal but to force, the vital principle and immediate parent of despotism; a well-disciplined militia, our best reliance in peace and for the first moments of war, till regulars may relieve them; the supremacy of the civil over the military authority; economy in the public expense, that labor may be lightly burdened; the honest payment of our debts and sacred preservation of public faith; encouragement of agriculture, and of commerce as its handmaid; the diffusion of information and arraignment of all abuses at the bar of the public reason; freedom of religion; freedom of the press, and freedom of person, under the protection of the habeas corpus, and trial by juries impartially selected. These principles form the bright constellation which has gone before us, and guided our steps through an age of revolution and reformation. The wisdom of our sages and blood of our heroes have been devoted to their attainment. They should be the creed of our political faith, the text of civic instruction, the touchstone by which to try the services of those we trust; and should we wander from them in moments of error or of alarm, let us hasten to retrace our steps and to regain the road which alone leads to peace, liberty, and safety.

I repair, then, fellow citizens, to the post you have assigned me. With experience enough in subordinate offices to have seen the difficulties of this the greatest of all, I have learned to expect that it will rarely fall to the lot of imperfect man to retire from this station with the reputation and the favor which bring him into it. Without pretensions to that high confidence you reposed in our first and greatest revolutionary character, whose preeminent services had entitled him to the first place in his country's love and destined for him the fairest page in the volume of faithful history, I ask so much confidence only as may give firmness and effect to the legal administration of your affairs. I shall often go wrong through defect of judgment. When right, I shall often be thought wrong by those whose positions will not command a view of the whole ground. I ask you indulgence for my own errors, which will never be intentional, and your support against the error of others, who may condemn what they would not if seen in all its parts. The approbation implied by your suffrage is a great consolation to me for the past, and my future solicitude will be to retain the good opinion of those who have bestowed it in advance, to conciliate that of others by doing them all the good in my power, and to be instrumental to the happiness and freedom of all.

Relying, then, on the patronage of your good will, I advance with obedience to the work, ready to retire from it whenever you become sensible how much better choice it is in your power to make. And may that Infinite Power which rules the destinies of the universe lead our councils to what is best, and give them a favorable issue for your peace and prosperity.

THOMAS JEFFERSON.

Letter to Thomas Ritchie

Martin Van Buren

January 13, 1827

T homas Ritchie was the editor of the Richmond Enquirer, which was one of
the most influential newspapers in the South. Van Buren contacted Ritchie
as part of Van Buren's effort to build the first true party organization in America
(see Document 9). Part of Van Buren's motivation was to prevent a repeat of the
disastrous results of the 1824 election when multiple candidates necessitated a
runoff election in the House of Representatives. Van Buren believed that a strong
party organization would produce a clear winner in the Electoral College.

Building on the remnants of the old Democratic-Republican Party, Van Buren
imagined a new party that would be more faithful to Jeffersonian principles. The
Democratic-Republicans had become too nationalist in their orientation and
threatened a return to Federalist principles. Van Buren tapped Andrew Jackson,
a military hero from the War of 1812, to be the standard bearer for the new Democratic Party, in hopes that his popularity would provide the necessary momentum
the party needed to secure victory.

The Democrats engaged in grassroots campaigning and began the process of
developing a national party organization. As part of that process, Van Buren
and the Democrats introduced the party convention to replace the party caucus
as a means of nominating presidential candidates. The conventions were far more
democratic and participatory than the caucus that had derisively become known
as "King Caucus."

Van Buren's efforts were rewarded when Jackson was elected president in 1828
and Van Buren was appointed secretary of state. Four years later, Van Buren was
selected as Jackson's running mate; in 1832, he was chosen to be Jackson's successor
to the presidency.

SOURCE: "Martin Van Buren, Letter to Thomas Ritchie, January 13, 1827," in *History of U.S.
Political Parties*, vol. 1, ed. Arthur Schlesinger (New York: Chelsea House, 1973), 539–541.

Dear Sir,

You will have observed an article in the *Argus* upon the subject of a national convention. That matter will soon be brought under discussion here and I sincerely wish you would bestow upon it some portion of your attention.... The following may, I think, justly be ranked among its probable advantages.

First, It is the best and probably the only practicable mode of concentrating the entire vote of the opposition and of effecting what is of still greater importance, the substantial re-organization of the Old Republican Party.

2nd Its first result cannot be doubtful. Mr. [John Quincy] Adams[1] occupying the seat and being determined not to surrender it except in extremis *will not submit his pretensions to the convention. Noah's[2]* real or affected apprehensions upon that subject are idle. I have long been satisfied that we can only get rid of the present, and restore a better state of things, by combining General Jackson's[3] personal popularity with the portion of old party feeling yet remaining. This sentiment is spreading, and would of itself be sufficient to nominate him at the Convention.

3rd. The call of such a convention, its exclusive Republican character, and the refusal of Mr. Adams and his friends to become parties to it, would draw anew the old Party lines and the subsequent contest would re-establish them; state nomination alone would fall far short of that object.

4th It would greatly improve the condition of the Republicans of the North & Middle States by substituting *party principle* for *personal preference* as one of the leading points in the contest. The location of the candidates would in a great degree be merged in its consideration. Instead of the question being between a Northern and Southern man, it would be whether or not the ties, which have heretofore bound together a great political party should be severed. The difference between the two questions would be found to be

---

[1] John Quincy Adams (1767–1848) began his political career as a diplomat, serving as minister to the Netherlands and then Prussia during his father's administration. He later served in the US Senate, then as secretary of state under James Monroe. He then won the highly contentious election of 1824, after which he would serve only one term of office.

[2] The "Noah" referenced here is likely Mordecai M. Noah, editor of the *Courier and Enquirer,* published in New York.

[3] Andrew Jackson (1767–1845) earned national fame as a war hero and would later become president of the United States, leading the country as its most influential and polarizing figure.

immense in the elective field. Altho' this is a mere party consideration it is
not on that account less likely to be effectual. Considerations of this character not infrequently operate as efficiently as those which bear upon the most
important questions of constitutional doctrine.

5thly It would place our Republican friends in New England on new and
strong grounds. They would have to decide between an indulgence in sectional and personal feeling with an entire separation from their old political
friends, on the one hand, or acquiescence in the fairly expressed will of the
party, on the other. In all the states the divisions between Republicans and
Federalists is still kept up and cannot be laid aside whatever the leaders of
the two parties may desire. Such a question would greatly disturb the democracy of the east.

6th. Its effects would be highly salutary on your section of the union by
the revival of old party distinctions. We must always have party distinctions
and the old ones are the best of which the nature of the case admits. Political
combinations between the inhabitants of the different states are unavoidable and the most natural and beneficial to the country is that between the
planters of the South and the plain Republicans of the north. The country has
once flourished under a party thus constituted and may again. It would take
longer than our lives (even if it were practicable) to create new party feelings
to keep those masses together. If the old ones are suppressed, geographical
divisions founded on local interests or, what is worse prejudices between
free and slaveholding states will inevitably take their place. Party attachment in former times furnished a complete antidote for sectional prejudices
by producing counteracting feelings. It was not until that defense had been
broken down that the clamor against Southern influence and African Slavery could be made effectual in the North. Those in the South who assisted in
producing the change are, I am satisfied, now deeply sensible of their error.
Formerly, attacks upon Southern Republicans were regarded by those of the
north as assaults upon their political brethren and resented accordingly. This
all powerful sympathy has been much weakened, if not, destroyed by the
amalgamating policy of Mr. Monroe.[4] It can and ought to be revived and the
proposed convention would be eminently serviceable in effecting that object.

---

[4] James Monroe (1758–1831) was the fifth United States president, known for overseeing westward expansion of the country and strengthening American foreign policy
in 1823 with the Monroe Doctrine, which warned European powers about further
colonization and intervention in the Western Hemisphere.

Lastly, the effect of such a nomination on General Jackson could not fail to be considerable. His election, as the result of his military services without reference to party and so far as he alone is concerned scarcely to principle would be one thing. His election as the result of a combined and concerted effort of a political party, holding in the main, to certain tenets and opposed to certain prevailing principles, might be another and a far different thing.

Autobiography

Martin Van Buren

c. 1854

M artin Van Buren (1782–1862) came of age in the rough-and-tumble world of New York party politics of the early 1800s and eventually became a major force in the state's democratic party. Known as the "Little Magician" because of his ability to make political victories appear against all odds, Van Buren headed up what was known as the New York Regency. The New York Regency was a new kind of political machine that made active use of the patronage (government jobs in exchange for political loyalty) to build strong party coalitions in support of candidates. Van Buren rejected the anti-party ideology of the founders and instead saw parties as a way in which individuals could pool resources to try to control the government. In addition, Van Buren not only defended the legitimacy of his own party but also advocated for the establishment of permanent opposition in politics, something that he saw as preventing the abuse of power and the creation of sectional prejudices.

As Van Buren transitioned into national politics, he took his party ideas to the national stage and played a major role in the establishment of a permanent two-party system in the United States. He was instrumental in the formation of the Democratic Party and convincing Andrew Jackson to attach himself to the new party organization. He would eventually succeed Jackson in office when he became president himself. Van Buren's emphasis on permanent opposition helped legitimize dissent and normalize the contentiousness of politics.

SOURCE: Martin Van Buren, *The Autobiography of Martin Van Buren*, ed. John C. Fitzpatrick (Washington: Government Printing Office, 1920), 123–126.

.... For the present it needs only to be stated that in the ranks of one or the other of these parties were arrayed almost all the People who took an interest in the management of public affairs. These differences were first developed in

Congress and in Society during the last term of Gen. Washington's[1] administration, had a partial and comparatively silent influence in the election of his successor,[2] but were openly proclaimed and maintained with much earnestness during that successor's entire administration. The result of this conflict of opinions was the expulsion of John Adams from the office of President and the election of Thomas Jefferson in his place. Not intolerant by nature Mr. Jefferson made an ineffectual effort to allay the warmth of these party differences and to prevent them from invading and poisoning the personal relations of individuals. But, true to his trust, he not only administered the government upon the principles for which a majority of the People had shown their preference, but he carried the spirit of that preference into his appointments to office to an extent sufficient to establish the predominance of those principles in every branch of the public service. This he did, not by way of punishing obnoxious opinions, or to gratify personal antipathies, but to give full effect to the will of the majority, submission to which he regarded as the vital principle of our Government.[3] Mr. [James] Madison,[4] elected by the same Party, tho' proverbial for his amiable temper and for the absence of anything like a proscriptive disposition, pursued the same course, and upon the same principle—the performance of a public trust in regard to the terms of which there was no room for doubt.

The Administrations of Jefferson and Madison, embracing a period of sixteen years, were, from first to last, opposed by the federal[5] party with a degree of violence unsurpassed in modern times. From this statement one of two conclusions must result. Either the conduct of these two parties which had been kept on foot so long, been sustained with such determined zeal and under such patriotic professions and had created distinctions that became the badges of families—transmitted from father to son—was a series of shameless impostures, covering mere struggles for power and patronage; or there were differences of opinion and principle between them of the greatest

---

[1] George Washington (1732–1799), president from 1789 to 1797.
[2] John Adams (1735–1826), president from 1797 to 1801.
[3] See Jefferson's First Inaugural Address, Document 7.
[4] James Madison (1751–1836) helped draft the Constitution and the Bill of Rights and served as president from 1809 to 1817.
[5] Van Buren does not capitalize "federal" in the original, perhaps as a slight to the Federalist Party whose politics were antithetical to his own. (Note that he does capitalize "Republican" when referring to the Democratic-Republican party led by Jefferson.) We are faithful to his choice throughout this text.

character, to which their respective devotion and active service could not be relaxed with safety or abandoned without dishonor. We should, I think, be doing great injustice to our predecessors if we doubted for a moment the sincerity of those differences, or the honesty with which they were entertained at least by the masses on both sides. The majority of the People, the sovereign power in our Government, had again and again, and on every occasion since those differences of opinion had been distinctly disclosed, decided them in favor of the Republican creed. That creed required only that unity among its friends should be preserved to make it the ark of their political safety. The Country had been prosperous and happy under its sway, and has been so through our whole history excepting only the period when it was convulsed and confounded by the criminal intrigues and commercial disturbances of the Bank of the United States.[6] To maintain that unity became the obligation of him whom its supporters had elevated to the highest place among its guardians. Jefferson and Madison so interpreted their duty. On the other hand, Mr. [James] Monroe,[7] at the commencement of his second term, took the ground openly, and maintained it against all remonstrances, that no difference should be made by the Government in the distribution of its patronage and confidence on account of the political opinions and course of applicants. The question was distinctly brought before him for decision by the Republican representatives from the states of Pennsylvania and New York, in cases that had deeply excited the feelings of their constituents and in which those constituents had very formally and decidedly expressed their opinions.

If the movement grew out of a belief that an actual dissolution of the federal party was likely to take place or could be produced by the course that was adopted, it showed little acquaintance with the nature of Parties to suppose that a political association that had existed so long, that had so many traditions to appeal to its pride, and so many grievances, real and fancied, to cry out for redness, could be disbanded by means of personal favors from the Executive or by the connivance of any of its leaders. Such has not

---

[6] Van Buren refers here to the Bank War when President Jackson vetoed an attempt by Congress to draw up a new charter for the bank. Jackson then removed all federal funds from the Second Bank of the United States, redistributing the funds to various state banks.

[7] James Monroe (1758–1831), the fifth US president, was known for overseeing westward expansion of the country and strengthening American foreign policy in 1823 with the Monroe Doctrine, which warned European powers about further colonization and intervention in the Western Hemisphere.

been the fate of long established political parties in any country. Their course may be qualified and their pretentions abated for a season by ill success, but the cohesive influences and innate qualities which originally united them remain with the mass and spring up in their former vigor with the return of propitious skies. Of this truth we need no more striking illustrations than are furnished by our own experience. Without going into the details of events familiar to all, I need only say that during the very "Era of Good Feelings,"[8] the federal party, under the names of federal republicans and whigs, elected their President over those old republicans William H. Crawford,[9] Andrew Jackson[10] and John C. Calhoun[11]—have, since his time twice elected old school federalists[12]—have possessed the most effective portions of the power of the Federal Government during their respective terms, with the exception, (if it was one) of the politically episodical administration of Vice President Tyler[13] and are at this time in power of the government of almost every free state. We shall find as a general rule that among the native inhabitants of each State, the politics of families who were federalists during the War of 1812, are the same now—holding, for the most part, under the name of Whigs, to the political opinions and governed by the feelings of their ancestors.

I have been led to take a more extended notice of this subject by my repugnance to a species of cant against Parties in which too many are apt to indulge when their own side is out of power and to forget when they come in. I have not, I think, been considered even by opponents as particularly rancorous in my party prejudices, and might not perhaps have anything to apprehend from a comparison, in this respect, with my contemporaries. But knowing, as all men of sense know, that political parties are inseparable from

---

[8] A popular term for the Monroe administration, referring to his attempt to quell partisanship.

[9] 1772–1834, former secretary of war and secretary of the treasury who ran for president in the 1824 election.

[10] 1767–1845, earned national fame as a war hero and would later become president of the United States, leading the country as its most influential and polarizing figure.

[11] 1782–1850, prominent statesman, senator, and spokesman for the slave-plantation system of the old South.

[12] We suspect Van Buren had William Henry Harrison and Zachary Taylor in mind here as these were the only Whig presidents elected in the era he describes.

[13] 1790–1862, tenth president of the US after being the tenth vice-president. Van Buren is likely alluding to the fact that Tyler was the first vice president to succeed to the presidency without an election. Tyler also had a falling out with his own Whig Party over policies he endorsed, having most of his cabinet resign and being formally expelled from the Whig Party.

free governments,[14] and that in many and material respects they are highly useful to the country, I never could bring myself for party purposes to deprecate their existence. Doubtless excesses frequently attend them and produce many evils, but not so many as are prevented by the maintenance of their organization and vigilance. The disposition to abuse power, so deeply planted in the human heart, can by no other means be more effectually checked; and it has always therefore struck me as more honorable and manly and more in harmony with the character of our People and of our Institutions to deal with the subject of Political Parties in a sincerer and wiser spirit—to recognize their necessity, to give them the credit they deserve, and to devote ourselves to improve and to elevate the principles and objects of our own and to support it ingenuously and faithfully. . . .

---

[14] Cf. *Federalist* 10 (Document 1) on the spirit of faction.

"House Divided" Speech

Abraham Lincoln

June 16, 1858

T*he "House Divided" speech was Lincoln's acceptance speech following the Illinois State Convention in Springfield nominating him as the Republican candidate for the United States Senate. It also turned out to be one of Lincoln's most controversial speeches: his opponent in the race, Stephen Douglas, interpreted it during their debates to be an abolitionist declaration. Abolition was not Lincoln's intention, however; Lincoln simply wanted to keep Republicans from going to Douglas's side after Douglas disavowed the Kansas-Lecompton Constitution. The Lecompton Constitution had been framed by Southern pro-slavery advocates in the territory of Kansas to try to get Kansas admitted as a pro-slavery state. This led some Republicans to see Douglas as a viable anti-slavery candidate. Lincoln therefore wanted to destroy Douglas' credibility on the slavery issue. In doing so, Lincoln also made allegations of a Democratic conspiracy to nationalize slavery and to extend its reach to every part of the Union.*

Sectional tension existed in America from the time of its founding. Delegates to the Constitutional Convention had managed this tension with a series of compromises written into the Constitution that made ratification possible and minimized conflict between North and South. But in the decades leading up to the secession crisis of 1860–61, disagreements between slaveholding and free states ballooned into major political crises. By the time of the Civil War, northerners saw in the South a society fundamentally shaped by the presence of slavery. Against this, white Southerners saw in the North an antagonistic and meddling people determined to undermine the South's slave-based social system.

It is little surprise that this sectional conflict would be reflected in America's political parties. Increasingly, the parties found themselves devoting large amounts of energy and political capital to managing the slavery tensions while at the same time brokering compromises to quell the growing conflict (e.g., the Compromise of 1850 and the Kansas-Nebraska Act of 1854). Eventually the strain grew too intense and snuffed out one political party (the Whigs), who could not internally manage the slavery issue, while dividing the other political party (the Democrats). Into this breach came a new political party, the Republicans, that opposed slavery and included a large number of abolitionists. The Republicans had no real following in the South and were perceived as a palpable threat by Southern whites. This new condition of the parties made compromise nearly impossible and sectional conflict all but inevitable.

SOURCE: Abraham Lincoln, "A Speech of the Hon. Abraham Lincoln," Illinois State Journal, vol. 11, no. 6, June 18, 1858. http://idnc.library.illinois.edu/?a=d&d=SJO18580618&e=
-------en-20--1--txt-txIN--------

Mr. PRESIDENT and Gentlemen of the Convention. If we could first know *where* we are, and *whither* we are tending, we could better judge *what* to do, and *how* to do it. We are now far into the *fifth* year, since a policy was initiated with the *avowed* object, and *confident* promise, of putting an end to slavery agitation. Under the operation of that policy, that agitation has not only, *not ceased*, but has *constantly augmented*. In *my* opinion, it *will* not cease, until a *crisis* shall have been reached and passed. "A house divided against itself cannot stand."[1] I believe this government cannot endure permanently half *slave* and half *free*. I do not expect the Union to be *dissolved*—I do not expect the house to *fall*—but I *do* expect it will cease to be divided. It will become *all* one thing, or *all* the other. Either the *opponents* of slavery, will arrest the further spread of it, and place it where the public mind shall rest in the belief that it is in the course of ultimate extinction; or its *advocates* will push it forward, till it shall become alike lawful in *all* the States, *old* as well as *new*—*North* as well as *South*.[2]

Have we no tendency to the latter condition?

Let anyone who doubts, carefully contemplate that now almost complete legal combination—piece of *machinery* so to speak—compounded of the Nebraska doctrine, and the Dred Scott decision.[3] Let him consider not only *what work* the machinery is adapted to do, and *how well* adapted; but

[1] Matthew 12:25.

[2] In referring to old and new states, Lincoln raises the issue of the expansion of slavery into the territories, which would eventually become slave states if they allowed slavery within their borders. The opposition to slavery in the territories was one of the key principles of the Republican Party.

[3] The Kansas-Nebraska Act, passed on May 30, 1854, allowed people in the territories of Kansas and Nebraska to decide for themselves whether or not to allow slavery within their borders. The *Dred Scott* decision was a Supreme Court case that held that a slave who had resided in a free state was not therefore entitled to his freedom,

also, let him study the *history* of its construction, and trace if he can, or rather *fail*, if he can, to trace the evidences of design, and concert of action, among its chief architects, from the beginning.

But, so far, *Congress* only, had acted; and an *indorsement* by the people, *real* or apparent, was indispensable, to *save* the point already gained, and give chance for more.

The new year of 1854 found slavery excluded from more than half the States by State Constitutions, and from most of the national territory by Congressional prohibition. Four days later, commenced the struggle, which ended in repealing that Congressional prohibition. This opened all the national territory to slavery; and was the first point gained.

This necessity had not been overlooked; but had been provided for, as well as might be, in the notable argument of *"squatter sovereignty,"* otherwise called *"sacred right of self government,"* which latter phrase, though expressive of the only rightful basis of any government, was so perverted in this attempted use of it as to amount to just this: That if any *one* man, choose to enslave *another*, no *third* man shall be allowed to object. That argument was incorporated into the Nebraska bill itself, in the language which follows: *"It being the true intent and meaning of this act not to legislate slavery into any Territory or State, nor to exclude it therefrom; but to leave the people thereof perfectly free to form and regulate their domestic institutions in their own way, subject only to the Constitution of the United States."* Then opened the roar of loose declamation in favor of "Squatter Sovereignty," and "Sacred right of self government."[4] "But," said opposition members, . . . "let us *amend* the bill so as to expressly declare that the people of the territory *may* exclude slavery." "Not we," said the friends of the measure; and down they voted the amendment.

. . . The election came. Mr. Buchanan was elected, and the *indorsement*, such as it was, secured. That was the *second* point gained. The indorsement, however, fell short of a clear popular majority by nearly four hundred thousand votes, and so, perhaps, was not overwhelmingly reliable and satisfactory. The *outgoing* President, in his last annual message, as impressively as possible *echoed back* upon the people the *weight* and *authority* of the indorsement. The Supreme Court met again; *did not* announce their decision, but ordered a reargument. The Presidential inauguration came, and still no decision of the

---

that blacks were not and could not be citizens of the United States, and that the Missouri Compromise was unconstitutional.

[4] This refers to Stephen Douglas's plan of popular sovereignty whereby individual territories are left to decide the slavery issue for themselves.

court; but the *incoming* President in his inaugural address, fervently exhorted the people to abide by the forthcoming decision, *whatever it might be*. Then, in a few days, came the decision.

The reputed author of the Nebraska bill finds an early occasion to make a speech at this capital indorsing the Dred Scott decision, and vehemently denouncing all opposition to it. The new President, too, seizes the early occasion of the Silliman letter to *indorse* and strongly *construe* that decision, and to express his *astonishment* that any different view had ever been entertained![5]

At length a squabble springs up between the President and the author of the Nebraska bill, on the *mere* question of *fact*, whether the Lecompton Constitution was or was not, in any just sense, made by the people of Kansas; and in that squabble the latter declares that all he wants is a fair vote for the people, and that he *cares* not whether slavery be voted *down* or voted *up*. I do not understand his declaration that he cares not whether slaver be voted down or voted up, to be intended by him other than as an *apt definition* of the *policy* he would impress upon the public mind—the *principle* for which he declares he has suffered so much, and is ready to suffer to the end. And well may he cling to that principle. If he has any parental feeling, well may he cling to it. That principle is the only *shred* left of his original Nebraska doctrine. Under the Dred Scott decision, "squatter sovereignty" squatted out of existence, tumbled down like temporary scaffolding—like the mold at the foundry served through one blast and fell back into loose sand—helped to carry an election, and then was kicked to the winds. His late *joint* struggle with the Republicans, against the Lecompton Constitution, involves nothing of the original Nebraska doctrine. That struggle was made on a point—the right of a people to make their own constitution,—upon which he and the Republicans have never differed.

The several points of the Dred Scott decision, in connection with Senator Douglas' "care not" policy, constitute the piece of machinery, in its *present* state of advancement.... The working points of that machinery are:—

---

[5] Yale professor Benjamin Sillman wrote a public letter condemning President Buchanan for sending Governor Robert Walker to Kansas with a military force to suppress the free state forces there. Although the facts were not quite right, Buchanan authored a terse reply, denying that there was any illegitimacy pertaining to the pro-slavery government, and stigmatizing the free states as lawless and seditious rebels. He even compared their actions to the Hartford Convention undertaken during the War of 1812.

First, That no negro slave, imported as such from Africa, and no descendant of such slave, can ever be a *citizen* of any State, in the sense of that term as used in the Constitution of the United States. This point is made in order to deprive the negro, in every possible event, of the benefit of that provision of the United States Constitution, which declares that "The citizens of each State shall be entitled to all privilege and immunities of citizens in the several States."

Secondly, that "subject to the Constitution of the United States," neither *Congress* nor a *Territorial Legislature* can exclude slavery from any United States territory. This point is made in order that individual men may *fill up* the territories with slaves, without danger of losing them as property, and thus to enhance the chances of *permanency* to the institution through all the future.

Thirdly, that whether the holding a negro in actual slavery in a free State, makes him free, as against the holder, the United States courts will not decide, but will leave to be decided by the courts of any slave State the negro may be forced into by the master. This point is made, not to be pressed *immediately*; but, if acquiesced in for a while, and apparently *indorsed* by the people at an election, *then* to sustain the logical conclusion that what Dred Scott's master might lawfully do with Dred Scott, in the free State of Illinois, every other master may lawfully do with any other *one*, or one *thousand* slaves, in Illinois, or in any other free State.

... We cannot absolutely know that all these exact adaptations are the result of preconcert. But when we see a lot of framed timbers, different portions of which we know have been gotten out at different times and places and by different workmen—Stephen, Franklin, Roger and James,[6] for instance—and when we see these timbers joined together, and see they exactly make the frame of a house or a mill, all the tenons and mortices exactly fitting, and all the lengths and proportions of the different pieces exactly adapted to their respective places, and not a piece too many or too few—not omitting even scaffolding—or, if a single piece be lacking, we see the place in the frame exactly fitted and prepared yet to bring such piece in—in such a case, we find it impossible not to believe that Stephen and Franklin and Roger and James all understood one another from the beginning, and all worked upon a common plan or draft drawn up before the first blow was struck....

---

[6] Stephen Douglas, Franklin Pierce, Roger Taney, and James Buchanan.

Letter to Henry Pierce and Others

Abraham Lincoln

April 6, 1859

H*aving gained public notice from the Lincoln-Douglas debates, Lincoln was invited by Henry Pierce, head of a committee of Boston Republicans, to attend a festival in honor of Thomas Jefferson's birthday. Lincoln was not able to attend the event but sent this letter instead, which was widely circulated in the Republican press. In the letter, he held up Jefferson's principles as the "definitions and axioms" of a free society and articulated his view that agreement on first principles was a necessary precondition to having civic discourse. His praise of Jefferson, a Democratic-Republican, rhetorically placed the Republican party as the true heir to the principles and values of American republicanism—a position often claimed by the Democratic Party. Both parties, of course, had a vested interest in claiming a lineage to Thomas Jefferson. Jefferson was revered as a towering figure of the founding generation, and celebrations would be held on his birthday. Showing that Jefferson's ideas and principles supported a given political party gave that party legitimacy and credibility in the eyes of Americans. This was particularly important for the still-nascent Republican Party that was trying to gain a foothold among the American electorate and in American politics.*

SOURCE: *Complete Works of Abraham Lincoln*, eds. John Nicolay and John Hay, vol. 2 (New York: Francis Tandy, 1905). https://quod.lib.umich.edu/l/lincoln/lincoln3/1:98? rgn=div1;view=fulltext.

Springfield, Ills., April 6, 1859

Messrs. Henry L. Pierce, & others.

Gentlemen

Your kind note inviting me to attend a Festival in Boston, on the 13th. Inst. in honor of the birth-day of Thomas Jefferson, was duly received. My engagements are such that I can not attend.

Bearing in mind that about seventy years ago, two great political parties were first formed in this country, that Thomas Jefferson was the head of one of them, and Boston the headquarters of the other, it is both curious and interesting that those supposed to descend politically from the party opposed to Jefferson should now be celebrating his birthday in their own original seat of empire, while those claiming political descent from him have nearly ceased to breathe his name everywhere.

Remembering too, that the Jefferson party was formed upon its supposed superior devotion to the *personal* rights of men, holding the rights of *property* to be secondary only, and greatly inferior, and then assuming that the so-called democracy of to-day, are the Jefferson, and their opponents, the anti-Jefferson parties, it will be equally interesting to note how completely the two have changed hands as to the principle upon which they were originally supposed to be divided.

The democracy of to-day hold the *liberty* of one man to be absolutely nothing, when in conflict with another man's right of *property*. Republicans, on the contrary, are for both the *man* and the *dollar*; but in cases of conflict, the man *before* the dollar.

I remember once being much amused at seeing two partially intoxicated men engage in a fight with their great-coats on, which fight, after a long, and rather harmless contest, ended in each having fought himself *out* of his own coat, and *into* that of the other. If the two leading parties of this day are really identical with the two in the days of Jefferson and Adams,[1] they have performed the same feat as the two drunken men.

But soberly, it is now no child's play to save the principles of Jefferson from total overthrow in this nation.

One would start with great confidence that he could convince any sane child that the simpler propositions of Euclid are true; but, nevertheless, he would fail, utterly, with one who should deny the definitions and axioms. The principles of Jefferson are the definitions and axioms of free society. And yet they are denied and evaded, with no small show of success. One dashingly calls them "glittering generalities";[2] another bluntly calls them "self evident lies";[3] and still others insidiously argue that they apply only to "superior races."[4]

---

[1] Lincoln is referring to the Democratic-Republicans and the Federalists.

[2] The reference here is to Rufus Choate from a public letter he wrote to the Maine Whig Committee.

[3] The "self-evident lies" quote is credited to Senator John Pettit of Indiana. More broadly, this phrase could also be associated with John Calhoun.

[4] Lincoln is likely referring to the ideas of Stephen Douglas here.

These expressions, differing in form, are identical in object and effect—the supplanting the principles of free government, and restoring those of classification, caste, and legitimacy. They would delight a convocation of crowned heads, plotting against the people. They are the van-guard—the miners, and sappers—of returning despotism. We must repulse them, or they will subjugate us.

This is a world of compensations; and he who would *be* no slave, must consent to *have* no slave. Those who deny freedom to others, deserve it not for themselves; and, under a just God, can not long retain it.

All honor to Jefferson—to the man who, in the concrete pressure of a struggle for national independence by a single people, had the coolness, forecast, and capacity to introduce into a merely revolutionary document, an abstract truth, applicable to all men and all times, and so to embalm it there, that to-day, and in all coming days, it shall be a rebuke and a stumbling-block to the very harbingers of re-appearing tyranny and oppression.

Your obedient servant,
A. LINCOLN—

Republican Party Platform of 1860

May 17, 1860

In 1860, the Republican Party met in Chicago. There was widespread speculation that William H. Seward would become the party's nominee, being
the best-known figure in the field. Other contenders included John McLean of
Ohio, Simon Cameron of Pennsylvania, Salmon P. Chase of Ohio, and Abraham Lincoln of Illinois. Seward's long tenure in politics, however, proved to be
his undoing. He had accumulated many enemies over the years, especially in the
South, and also faced stiff opposition from forces in the North, in particular the
Know-Nothings. He had also characterized the dispute between North and South
as an "irrepressible conflict" and this made him seem a poor choice for handling
relations between the sections. In contrast, Lincoln's star was on the rise. He had
gained a national reputation from the debates he held with Stephen Douglas
during the 1858 Illinois senatorial campaign (see Document 10) and was willing
to call slavery the evil that it was. By the third ballot, Lincoln had gained enough
votes to secure the party's nomination and would go on to win the election over
his Democratic opponents.

　　Lincoln had become widely known for his anti-slavery stance and seemed to fit
solidly into a political party that abhorred slavery and wanted to see it eradicated.
Democrats, especially Southerners, depicted the Republicans as an abolition party
and issued dire warnings that Lincoln would take action to free the slaves if elected
president. Lincoln, on the other hand, claimed to have no power as president to
free the slaves, although he asserted presidential authority to block the spread of
slavery into the territories.

SOURCE: Platform Adopted by the National Republican Convention, held in Chicago, May
17, 1860. Library of Congress, http://hdl.loc.gov/loc.rbc/lprbscsm.scsm0716.

Resolved, That we, the delegated representatives of the Republican electors
of the United States, in Convention assembled, in discharge of the duty we
owe to our constituents and our country, unite in the following declarations:

The Republican Party.

1. That the history of the nation during the last four years, has fully established the propriety and necessity of the organization and perpetuation of the Republican party, and that the causes which called it into existence are permanent in their nature, and now, more than ever before, demand its peaceful and constitutional triumph.

Its Fundamental Principles.

2. That the maintenance of the principles promulgated in the Declaration of Independence and embodied in the Federal Constitution, "That all men are created equal; that they are endowed by their Creator with certain inalienable rights; that among these are life, liberty, and the pursuit of happiness; that to secure these rights, governments are instituted among men, deriving their just powers from the consent of the governed"—is essential to the preservation of our Republican institutions; and that the Federal Constitution, the Rights of the States, and the Union of the States must and shall be preserved.

True to the Union.

3. That to the Union of the States, this nation owes its unprecedented increase of population, its surprising development of material resources, its rapid augmentation of wealth, its happiness at home and its honor abroad; and we hold in abhorrence all schemes for Disunion, come from whatever source they may: And we congratulate the country that no Republican member of Congress has uttered or countenanced the threats of Disunion so often made by Democratic members, without rebuke and with applause from their political associates; and we denounce those threats of Disunion, in case of a popular overthrow of their ascendancy as denying the vital principles of a free government, and as an avowal of contemplated treason, which it is the imperative duty of an indignant People sternly to rebuke and forever silence.

State Sovereignty.

4. That the maintenance inviolate of the Rights of the States, and especially the right of each State to order and control its own domestic institutions according to its own judgment exclusively, is essential to that balance of

power on which the perfection and endurance of our political fabric depends; and we denounce the lawless invasion by armed force of the soil of any State or Territory, no matter under what pretext, as among the gravest of crimes.

Sectionalism of the Democracy.

5. That the present Democratic Administration has far exceeded our worst apprehensions, in its measureless subserviency to the exactions of a sectional interest, as especially evinced in its desperate exertions to force the infamous Lecompton Constitution upon the protesting people of Kansas; in construing the personal relation between master and servant to involve an unqualified property in persons; in its attempted enforcement, everywhere, on land and sea, through the intervention of Congress and of the Federal Courts, of the extreme pretensions of a purely local interest; and in its general and unvarying abuse of power entrusted to it by a confiding people.

Its Extravagance and Corruption.

6. That the people justly view with alarm the reckless extravagance which pervades every department of the Federal Government; that a return to rigid economy and accountability is indispensable to arrest the systematic plunder of the public treasury by favored partisans; while the recent startling developments of frauds and corruptions at the Federal metropolis, show that an entire change of administration is imperatively demanded.

A Dangerous Political Heresy.

7. That the new dogma that the Constitution, of its own force, carries Slavery into any or all of the Territories of the United States, is a dangerous political heresy, at variance with the explicit provisions of that instrument itself, with cotemporaneous exposition, and with legislative and judicial precedent; is revolutionary in its tendency, and subversive of the peace and harmony of the country.

Freedom, the Normal Condition of Territories.

8. That the normal condition of all the territory of the United States is that of Freedom: That as our Republican fathers, when they had abolished slavery in all our national territory, ordained that "no person should be deprived of

life, liberty, or property, without due process of law," it becomes our duty, by legislation, whenever such legislation is necessary, to maintain this provision of the Constitution against all attempts to violate it; and we deny the authority of Congress, of a territorial legislature, or of any individuals, to give legal existence to slavery in any Territory of the United States.

The African Slave Trade.

9. That we brand the recent re-opening of the African Slave Trade, under the cover of our national flag, aided by perversions of judicial power, as a crime against humanity and a burning shame to our country and age; and we call upon Congress to take prompt and efficient measures for the total and final suppression of that execrable traffic.

Democratic Popular Sovereignty.

10. That in the recent vetoes, by their Federal Governors, of the acts of the Legislatures of Kansas and Nebraska, prohibiting Slavery in those Territories, we find a practical illustration of the boasted Democratic principle of Non-Intervention and Popular Sovereignty embodied in the Kansas-Nebraska Bill, and a demonstration of the deception and fraud involved therein.

Admission of Kansas.

11. That Kansas should, of right, be immediately admitted as a State under the Constitution recently formed and adopted by her people, and accepted by the House of Representatives.

Encouragement of American Industry.

12. That, while providing revenue for the support of the general government by duties upon imports, sound policy requires such an adjustment of these imports as to encourage the development of the industrial interests of the whole country; and we commend that policy of national exchanges, which secures to the working men liberal wages, to agriculture remunerating prices, to mechanics and manufacturers an adequate reward for their skill, labor and enterprise, and to the nation commercial prosperity and independence.

Free Homesteads.

13. That we protest against any sale or alienation to others of the Public Lands held by actual settlers, and against any view of the Free Homestead policy which regards the settlers as paupers or suppliants for public bount; and we demand the passage by Congress of the complete and satisfactory Homestead Measure which has already passed the House.

Rights of Citizenship.

14. That the Republican party is opposed to any change in our Naturalization Laws or any State Legislation by which the rights of citizenship hitherto accorded to emigrants from foreign lands shall be abridged or impaired; and in favor of giving a full and efficient protection to the rights of all classes of citizens, whether native or naturalized, both at home and abroad.

River and Harbor Improvements.

15. The appropriations by Congress for River and Harbor improvements of a National character, required for the accommodation and security of an existing commerce, are authorized by the Constitution, and justified by the obligation of Government to protect the lives and property of its citizens.

A Pacific Railroad.

16. That a Railroad to the Pacific Ocean is imperatively demanded by the interests of the whole country; that the Federal Government ought to render immediate and efficient aid in its construction; and that, as preliminary thereof, a daily Overland Mail should be promptly established.

Co-operation Invited.

17. Finally, having thus set forth our distinctive principles and views, we invite the co-operation of all citizens, however differing on other questions, who substantially agree with us in their affirmance and support.

Democratic Party Platform 1860 (Douglas Faction)

(Northern) Democratic Party Platform Committee

June 18, 1860

In April of 1860, Democrats met in Charleston, South Carolina, to select their nominee. At that time, Charleston was a city overrun by secessionist passions, and with no local Whig party presence since earlier in the century, there was nothing to dampen those passionate excesses. Disagreement over the platform caused Southern delegates to withdraw from the convention after delegates affiliated with Stephen Douglas refused to concede to any platform that did not support popular sovereignty. The question of the nominee and the platform was left unresolved as Douglas could not secure the two-thirds majority needed to win.

In June of 1860, Democrats reconvened in Baltimore to try to settle their differences. Secessionists reappeared at the convention and a great deal of infighting took place over the seating of rival delegations. When the Douglas supporters won, Southerners again left the convention, and the remaining delegates nominated Stephen Douglas for the presidency. Senator Benjamin Fitzpatrick of Alabama was initially selected for the vice presidency, but he declined. Instead, a Georgia moderate named Herschel Johnson was selected for the position.

SOURCE: Democratic Party Platform 1860 (Douglas Faction), June 18, 1860. Online by Gerhard Peters and John T. Woolley, *The American Presidency Project.* https://www.presidency.ucsb.edu/node/273172.

Resolved, That we, the Democracy of the Union, in Convention assembled, do hereby declare our affirmation of the resolutions unanimously adopted and declared as a platform of principles by the Democratic Convention at Cincinnati, in the year 1856, believing that Democratic principles are unchangeable in their nature when applied to the same subject matters; and we recommend, as the only further resolutions, the following:

Inasmuch as difference of opinion exists in the Democratic party as to the nature and extent of the powers of a Territorial Legislature, and as to the powers and duties of Congress, under the Constitution of the United States, over the institution of slavery within the territories,

Resolved, That the Democratic party will abide by the decision of the Supreme Court of the United States upon these questions of Constitutional law.

Resolved, That it is the duty of the United States to afford ample and complete protection to all citizens, whether at home or abroad, and whether native or foreign born.

Resolved, That one of the necessities of the age, in a military, commercial and postal point of view is speedy communication between the Atlantic and Pacific States, and the Democratic party pledge such constitutional power of the Government as will insure the construction of a railroad to the Pacific coast at the earliest practicable period.

Resolved, That the Democratic party are in favor of the acquisition of Cuba on such terms as shall be honorable to ourselves and just to Spain.

Resolved, That the enactments of State Legislatures to defeat the faithful execution of the Fugitive Slave Law, are hostile in character and subversive to the Constitution, and revolutionary in their effects.

Resolved, That it is in accordance with the Cincinnati Platform that during the existence of Territorial Governments the measure of restriction, whatever it may be, imposed by the Federal Constitution on the power of the Territorial Legislature over the subject of the domestic relations, as the same has been, or shall hereafter be finally determined by the Supreme Court of the United States, should be respected by all good citizens, and enforced with promptness and fidelity by every branch of the General Government.

Democratic Party Platform 1860 (Breckinridge Faction)

(Southern) Democratic Party Platform Committee

November 6, 1860

When the Democratic Party met in Baltimore in 1860 to try to overcome their differences, infighting between the different factions was intense and bitter (see Document 13). Northern Democrats supported Stephen Douglas and wanted a platform that emphasized the principle of popular sovereignty for the territories. Douglas's opposition to the recognition of Kansas, however, had made him deeply unpopular in the South, and Southerners demanded a platform that called for direct constitutional protection for slavery in the territories. When it became clear that the two sides could not be reconciled and that Douglas's supporters had the upper hand, Southerners stormed out of the convention vowing to go it alone. Conventions of Southerners were held in Baltimore and in Richmond. In both cities, southern Democrats nominated John Breckinridge of Kentucky for president and Joseph Lane of Oregon for vice president. Southerners favoring secession cheered the party split, paving the way toward the breakup of the Union with Lincoln's election.

SOURCE: Democratic Party Platform 1860 (Breckinridge Faction), November 6, 1860. Online by Gerhard Peters and John T. Woolley, *The American Presidency Project*. https://www.presidency.ucsb.edu/node/273278.

Resolved, That the platform adopted by the Democratic party at Cincinnati is affirmed, with the following explanatory resolutions:

First—That the government of a Territory organized by an act of Congress is provisional and temporary, and during its existence all citizens of the United States have an equal right to settle with their property in the Territory, without their rights, either of person or property, being destroyed or injured by Congressional or Territorial legislation.

Second—That it is the duty of the Federal Government, in all its departments, to protect, when necessary, the rights of the persons and property in the Territories, and wherever else its constitutional authority extends.

Third—That when the settlers in a Territory, having an adequate population, form a State Constitution, the right of sovereignty commences, and being consummated by admission into the Union, they stand on an equal footing with the people of other States; and a State thus organized ought to be admitted into the Federal Union, whether its Constitution prohibits or recognizes the institution of slavery.

Resolved, That the Democratic party are in favor of the acquisition of the island of Cuba, on such terms as shall be honorable to ourselves and just to Spain, at the earliest practicable moment.

Resolved, That the enactments of State Legislatures to defeat the faithful execution of the Fugitive Slave Law, are hostile in character to, and subversive of, the Constitution, and revolutionary in their effect.

Resolved, That the Democracy of the United States recognize it as an imperative duty of the Government to protect naturalized citizens in all their rights, whether at home or in foreign lands, to the same extent as its native-born citizens.

Whereas, One of the greatest necessities of the age, in a political, commercial, postal, and military point of view, is a speedy communication between the Pacific and Atlantic coasts; therefore, be it

Resolved, That the National Democratic party do hereby pledge themselves to use every means in their power to secure the passage of some bill, to the extent of the constitutional authority of Congress, for the construction of a Pacific Railroad from the Mississippi River or the Pacific Ocean, at the earliest practicable moment.

"The Coming Woman"

Victoria C. Woodhull

April 2, 1870

W hen Victoria Woodhull launched her campaign for the presidency,
women were still fifty years away from having the right to vote. Throughout her life, however, Woodhull had pushed back against the limitations American society placed on women. With her sister, Tennessee Claflin, she owned a
successful stock brokerage; shortly after announcing her intention to seek the
office of the presidency, the two began editing and publishing a weekly newspaper to provide coverage of her campaign. Two years after her announcement,
Woodhull was officially nominated to be the presidential candidate for the Equal
Rights Party, with Frederick Douglass as her vice president. Although Woodhull's presidential bid was ultimately unsuccessful, her candidacy raised the
profile of woman's rights as an issue to be taken seriously by other national
political parties.

SOURCE: Victoria Woodhull, "The Coming Woman," March 29, 1870, *New York Herald*, p. 8.
https://www.newspapers.com/clip/6836678/victoria_woodhull_announces_her/.

TO THE EDITOR OF THE HERALD:—

The disorganized condition of parties in the United States at the present
time affords a favorable opportunity for a review of the political situation
and for comment on the issues which are likely to come up for settlement
in the Presidential election in 1872. As I happen to be the most prominent
representative of the only unrepresented class in the republic, and perhaps
the most practical exponent of the principles of equality; I request the favor
of being permitted to address the public through the medium of the *Herald*.
While others of my sex devoted themselves to a crusade against the laws that
shackle the women of the country, I asserted my individual independence;
while others prayed for the time coming, I worked for it; while others argued
the equality of woman with man, I proved it by successfully engaging in

business; while others sought to show that there was no valid reason why woman should be treated socially and politically as a being inferior to man, I boldly entered the arena of politics and business and exercised the rights I already possessed. I therefore claim the right to speak for the unenfranchised women of the country, and believing as I do that there will be

MORE FEMALE OFFICEHOLDERS
THAN FEMALE VOTERS[1]

for some time to come, and that the prejudices that still exist in the popular mind against women in public life will soon disappear, I now announce myself as a candidate for the Presidency. I am quite well aware that in assuming this position I shall evoke more ridicule than enthusiasm at the outset. But this is an epoch of sudden changes and startling surprises[:] What may appear absurd to-day will assume a serious aspect to-morrow. I am content to wait until my claim for recognition as a candidate shall receive the calm consideration of the press and the public. The blacks were cattle in 1800; a negro now sits in Jeff Davis' seat in the United States Senate.[2] The sentiment of the country was, even in 1863, against negro suffrage; now the negro's right to vote is acknowledged by a majority of the States, and will soon be recognized by the Constitution of the United States. Let those, therefore, who ridiculed the negro's claim to exercise the right to "life, liberty and the pursuit of happiness," and lived to see him vote and hold high public offices, ridicule the aspirations of the women of the country after equality with the blacks as much as they please. They cannot roll back the rising tide of reform.

---

[1] Woodhull refers to the fact that while women were often explicitly precluded from voting, many statutes listing the qualifications for office were silent on the question of sex. Women's rights advocates therefore began to run for elected offices in the 1850s in part to highlight the absurdity of being able to vote for a woman in an election where no woman could cast a vote. Interestingly, these enterprising female candidates were occasionally successful: see the database compiled by Wendy E. Chmielewski, Jill Norgren, and Kristen Gwinn-Becker, "Her Hat Was In The Ring: U.S. Women Who Ran for Political Office before 1920," at http://www.herhatwasin thering.org/.
[2] Hiram Rhodes Revels (1827–1901) represented Mississippi in the US Senate from 1870 to 1871. A Republican, he was the first African American to serve in Congress.

THE WORLD MOVES.

That great governmental changes were to follow the enfranchisement of the negro I have long foreseen. While the curse of slavery covered the land progress was enchained, but when it was swept away in the torrent of war the voice of justice was heard, and it became evident that the last weak barrier against complete political and social equality must soon give way. All that has been said and written hitherto in support of

EQUALITY FOR WOMEN

has had its proper effect on the public mind, just as the anti-slavery speeches before secession were effective; but a candidate and a policy are required to prove it. Lincoln's election showed the strength of the feeling against the peculiar institution; my candidacy for the Presidency will, I confidently expect, develop the fact that the principles of equal rights for all have taken deep root. The advocates of political equality for women have, besides a respectable known strength, a great undercurrent of unexpected power, which is only awaiting a fit opportunity to show itself. By the general and decided test, I propose we shall be able to understand the woman question aright, or at least shall have done much toward presenting

THE ISSUE INVOLVED

in proper shape. I claim to possess the strength and courage to be the subject of that test and look forward confidently of a triumphant issue of the canvass.

The present position of political parties is anomalous. They are not inspired by any great principles of policy or economy. Political preachers paw the air; there is no live issue up for discussion. The only seemingly distinctive feature upon which a complete and well-defined diversion exists is on the dead issue of negro equality, and this is to the political leaders

A HARP OF A THOUSAND STRINGS.

The minor questions of the hour do not affect parties as such, and no well-defined division of sentiment exists. A great national question is wanted to prevent a descent into pure sectionalism. The simple issue whether women should not have political equality with the negro is the only one to be tried, and none more important is likely to arise before the Presidential election. But beside the question of equality others of great magnitude are necessarily included. The platform that is to succeed in the coming election must enunciate the general principles of

ENLIGHTENED JUSTICE AND ECONOMY.

A complete reform in our system of prison discipline, having specially in view the welfare of the families of criminals, whose labor should not be lost to them; the rearrangement of the system and control of internal improvements; the adoption of some better means for caring for the helpless and indigent; the establishment of strictly mutual and reciprocal relations with all foreign Powers who will unite to better the condition of the productive class, and the adoption of such principles as shall recognize this class as

THE TRUE WEALTH OF THE COUNTRY

and give it a just position beside capital, thus introducing a practical plan for universal government—these important changes can only be expected to follow a complete departure from the beaten tracks of political parties and their machinery; and this, I believe, my canvass of 1872 will effect.

That the people are sick of the present administration is a proposition, I think, that does not require to be argued; but as I have now taken a decided stand against its continuance for another term of four years, and offered myself as a candidate for the Presidential succession, a few preliminary observations on the general management of

OUR HOME AND FOREIGN POLICY

will not be out place. The administration of General Grant then, has been a failure from the beginning; weak, vacillating and deficient in moral courage, it commands neither the respect nor admiration of foreign Powers nor receives the active support of its party. The general management of our foreign and domestic affairs does not seem to me to have risen to the dignity of a policy, though it be allowed to have been consistent in its various parts. It has been destitute of that decision and firmness that characterize the victorious soldier who is now President. A decided Cuban policy would not only have settled at once the inevitable destiny of that island, but would also have given republican sentiment in Spain an impetus, strengthened the South American republics and exercised a healthy influence in Mexico and Canada. But instead of this we have to submit to the consequences of

A POLICY OF COWARDICE

American citizens abroad are murdered by Spanish cutthroats,[3] our consuls are insulted, our flag is disgraced. This is unworthy of the American nation, and the people will hold Grant accountable. A giant who never shows his strength is neither feared nor respected. On the important questions of taxation, the tariff and the public debt the administration seems to have no settled policy. Taxation, whether for the support of the government or the payment of the debt, should in all cases be general and never special. No special interest, nor several special interests, should be singled out to sustain an extra proportion of taxation. And in regard to the tariff the same principle should be enforced. Whether the public debt be a blessing or a curse, it exists. Created to save the republic, it must be paid strictly according to both the spirit and the letter of the law. But there is no immediate necessity for paying it off. By a proper policy its payment might be made to extend through a hundred years, for even beyond that time will the benefits its creation produced be felt and appreciated. In older countries the pressure of national debt becomes a heavier charge and a more mighty burden every succeeding year, but with us the very reverse is the case. The development of our magnificent resources will render the gradual payment of our indebtedness easy of accomplishment.

ALL OTHER QUESTIONS,

whether of a foreign or domestic nature, stand illustrated by the Cuban policy of the administration. A bold, firm and, withal, consistent national policy, if not at all times strictly within the conservative limits of international law will always command the respect and support of the people.

With the view of taking the people into my confidence I have written several papers on governmental questions of importance and will submit them in due time. For the present the foregoing must suffice. I anticipate criticism;

---

[3] Woodhull refers here to the Virginius Affair in which an American ship was hired by Cuban insurrectionists to send men and munitions to Cuba to make war on the Spanish. The ship was captured by the Spanish and fifty-three men were executed before Britain intervened and stopped the killings.

but however unfavorable the comment this letter may evoke I trust that my sincerity will not be called in question. I have deliberately and of my own accord placed myself before the people as a candidate for the Presidency of the United States, and saving the means, courage, energy and strength necessary for the race intend to contest it to the close.

VICTORIA C. WOODHULL.

"Wanted—A Party"

Woodrow Wilson

September 1, 1886

W oodrow Wilson took an untraditional route to politics. He earned a doc-
torate from Johns Hopkins University in 1886 and took a teaching position
in the politics department at Princeton University in 1890. In 1902, he became
president of Princeton. He was then elected governor of New Jersey in 1910 and
became the Democratic nominee for the presidency in 1912.

Wilson wrote extensively about American politics and believed that many
flaws existed in the American political system. In particular, Wilson was quite
critical of America's political parties which he believed did not provide voters with
clear choices on policies. He was also critical of the separation of powers and felt
that the separation did not allow for an alignment of purpose and action between
the executive and legislative branches. The solution he proposed was for stronger
political parties to bring harmony between the different branches and to allow
coordinating action to take place.

SOURCE: Woodrow Wilson, "Wanted—A Party," September 1, 1886, published in the *Boston*
Times, September 27, 1886.

A man must nowadays either belong to a party through mere force of habit,
or else be puzzled to know what party he belongs to. Party platforms furnish
no sort of chart by which he can shape his political course. Unless they are
carefully labelled, he cannot tell which party speaks through them, for they
all say much the same thing. If voters chose their party instead of happening into it, they would probably choose by the aid of two questions, namely,
first, "What policy do we favor?" and, second, "Which party advocates that
policy?" Perhaps it is fortunate, therefore, that so many drift to the ballot-box
and so few choose; for, otherwise, multitudes would lose their votes before
answering the second of these questions. They would practically disfranchise
themselves if they waited to answer it. The professions of existing parties do
not furnish any satisfactory reply to it; still less do their actions. Does anyone

favor civil service reform? The present act establishing competitive examinations and a commission was proposed by a democratic senator to a republican senate, was passed by that body and a democratic house, and signed by a republican president.[1] The senator who proposed it was afterward cast aside by his constituency because of his reform sentiments. His measure is now administered with full sympathy for its purposes, by a democratic president elected because of his record on this question; but it is covertly attacked in a democratic house, and openly sneered at in a republican senate; and the democratic chairman of the house committee on civil service reform fails of a renomination in North Carolina because of his fine reform work on that committee.[2] Which party, then, advocates civil service reform?

... But why extend the perplexing recital? It is sadly confounding to think about so much confusion. And, be it observed, I am not speaking of these things in ridicule of our national parties, or in disgust with our national politics, nor yet in despair of our national institutions. I am simply gathering facts to serve as food for reflection, and in order to state what my own reflections upon them have been. My chief reflection has been ... that such a course of things is tending, so to say, to *individualize* our politics....

First, let me explain what I mean by the individualizing of our politics. I mean simply that the voter who exercises any choice at all, is being obliged to choose *men*, particular individuals, to tie to, instead of parties. Of course, the conscientious voter always choses between men, between candidates, in voting; but formerly he could choose them as representing parties. Now he must choose them instead of parties. The feeling is: "No party means what it says; some men do seem to mean what they say; we will tie to them when we can." The last presidential election of course furnishes the most striking illustration of the operation of this feeling. The mugwump[3] is the man who has cast loose from parties, which don't mean what they say, and offers to follow men who do speak with a purpose. Mr. Cleveland[4] is a democrat. But he was not elected because he was a democrat, but because the civil service of

---

[1] The Pendleton Act was introduced into the Senate by Democratic Senator George Pendleton (Ohio) and was signed into law by President Chester A. Arthur, who had ascended to the presidency after the assassination of President James A. Garfield. Passage of the act reduced Pendleton's popularity in Ohio, and he was not nominated for another term as senator.

[2] The new president was Democrat Grover Cleveland.

[3] Republican voters who bolted the party in the election of 1884 in response to corruption and opposition to the Republican nominee James Blaine.

[4] Served as the 22nd and 24th president of the United States.

the country needed reforming, and he evidently meant to reform it, if given a chance. A man of that sort in the presidential chair would be worth any number of party platforms; a great number of discriminating voters accordingly followed him in preference to any party—"irrespective of party," to use the orthodox phrase.

Mr. Cleveland's case was only a conspicuous one, however; it was not isolated. There is a yearly increasing number of mayors, governors, and congressmen holding their offices because of personal qualities or opinions pleasing to constituencies who do not stop to ask, in choosing them, whether the parties they formally represent possess like qualities or opinions.

Various reasons, historical and others, might be offered to explain this interesting but necessarily transitional state of affairs; as, for instance, that the republican party has outlived the purposes for which it was organized, and that the democratic party has ceased to be opposed to it in most matters, except in a Pickwickian[5] sense. The republican party rendered the country some inestimable services, and the country, in natural gratitude, pensioned it with a quarter of a century of power. Meantime, the democratic party kicked its heels with what philosophy it could command on the cold outside of the offices, comforting itself with dignified repetitions of certain old and important constitutional principles which had all of a sudden apparently lost their old power as charms to conjure with. But the republican pension has run out now. It could not reasonably be claimed for a second generation. The pensioners, too, got intolerable as they grew old. We, accordingly, have a president who is a democrat in favor of civil service reform, and a congress which is nothing in a particular and in favor of nothing unanimously, save large expenditures of money. The old parties, to put it in the vernacular, have "played out," and we are choosing here a man and there a man who means what he says, while waiting for a party which shall mean what *it* says.

The new parties which are hoped for in the future do not form readily or quickly for the same reason that the old parties have not adapted themselves to changed circumstances. Our system of government has supplied no official place, no place of actual authority, for leaders of parties. A party, consequently, must be merely a fortuitous concourse of atoms; and we must wait on the atoms. Even after it is formed, any party of ours must keep together rather by grace and enthusiasm than by vital organization. There is no ruling

---

[5] Taken from Charles Dickens's first novel, *The Posthumous Papers of the Pickwick Club,* which dealt with the inequities of the justice system. The book became quite popular, inspiring theatrical adaptations and related merchandise.

station in the government for its leaders. It must follow them rather for what they eloquently profess than for anything that they can actually do. The most leader-like post in politics is the speakership of the house of representatives, which is the most unsuitable place possible for a party captain. If we did not have a natural talent for forming parties, and it were not the fashion in all popular governments to have parties, it is to be seriously doubted whether we would not approximate that "natural society," of which some philosophers and some anarchists have dreamed, in which everybody would act for himself and nobody act, except accidentally, or through chance amiability, in concert with his neighbors.

There is, however, another and a better reason why we always have parties, and that is, that we have a splendid habit of all believing in certain great principles of human liberty and self-government, without being tamely all of one mind about the way in which those principles ought to be applied in particular cases. No time was ever bigger than this with unsolved problems as to the best ways in which to make liberty real and government helpful. Labor questions, financial questions, administrative questions must all tax the best thought of the country from this time on, until some clear purpose of reform, of financial reconstruction, or of governmental betterment is conceived by some group of men who mean what they say, who all mean the same thing, and who know how to say it, begin to speak their purpose, so that the nation will wake as at a new voice—a voice which calls with authority to duty and to action. Then a new party will be formed—and another party opposed to it. All that is wanting is a new, genuine and really meant purpose held by a few strong men of principle and boldness. That is a big "all," and it is still conspicuously wanting.

But the generations that really loved the old and now disintegrated parties is fast passing away. It is largely the new generation that wonders that anyone ever doubted that the war was over—even sometimes wonders what the war was all about—that is compelling a clearing away of the worn-out formulas of the old dispensation and a hastening of something not stated to determine their politics. With the growth of this new generation we shall unquestionably witness the growth of new parties.

DOCUMENT 17

Populist Party Platform 1892

July 4, 1892

T he Populists had emerged as a viable third party in the 1890 midterm elections when they captured nine congressional seats and won impressive victories in state and local politics. In general, the Populists reflected a growing
consensus among farmers that national policies favored industrial development
at the expense of agrarian concerns, and that the major parties had abandoned
the interests of small farmers. Republicans were immediately targeted for their
support of the "moneyed" power in the Northeast, but Democrats in the South
were also put on notice as small farmers in the South chafed under patrician rule.
The Populists wished to guarantee farm income through certain kinds of government regulation. More importantly, Populists began to insist on free silver and
monetary inflation as a way to relieve heavy mortgage burdens.

As the party met in Omaha to launch its first national campaign for the presidency, delegates disagreed on tactics and demands but were united in their enthusiasm and desire for reform. The platform was a mixture of altruism and practical
politics, displaying a desire to win combined with hope for a better future. Though
their presidential aspirations were unsuccessful, the Populists set the stage for the
candidacy of William Jennings Bryan in 1896.

SOURCE: Populist Party Platform 1892, July 4, 1892. Online by Gerhard Peters and John T.
Woolley, *The American Presidency Project.* https://www.presidency.ucsb.edu/node/273285.

———————————————

Assembled upon the 116th anniversary of the Declaration of Independence,
the People's Party[1] of America, in their first national convention, invoking
upon their action the blessing of Almighty God, put forth in the name and

———————————

[1] The People's Party was the initial name given to the movement; later, the party
changed its name to the Populist Party, a term coined by a writer for an Ohio
newspaper.

on behalf of the people of this country, the following preamble and declaration of principles:

PREAMBLE.

The conditions which surround us best justify our co-operation; we meet
in the midst of a nation brought to the verge of moral, political, and material
ruin. Corruption dominates the ballot-box, the Legislatures, the Congress,
and touches even the ermine[2] of the bench. The people are demoralized; most
of the States have been compelled to isolate the voters at the polling places
to prevent universal intimidation and bribery. The newspapers are largely
subsidized or muzzled, public opinion silenced, business prostrated, homes
covered with mortgages, labor impoverished, and the land concentrating in
the hands of capitalists. The urban workmen are denied the right to organize for self-protection, imported pauperized labor beats down their wages,
a hireling standing army, unrecognized by our laws, is established to shoot
them down, and they are rapidly degenerating into European conditions.[3]
The fruits of the toil of millions are boldly stolen to build up colossal fortunes
for a few, unprecedented in the history of mankind; and the possessors of
those, in turn, despise the Republic and endanger liberty. From the same
prolific womb of governmental injustice we breed the two great classes—
tramps and millionaires.

The national power to create money is appropriated to enrich bondhold-
ers; a vast public debt payable in legal tender currency has been funded into
gold-bearing bonds, thereby adding millions to the burdens of the people.

Silver, which has been accepted as coin since the dawn of history, has been
demonetized to add to the purchasing power of gold by decreasing the value
of all forms of property as well as human labor, and the supply of currency
is purposely abridged to fatten usurers, bankrupt enterprise, and enslave

---

[2] Ermine are weasels whose white fur and black-tipped tails have traditionally been
used to trim the edges of the ceremonial cloaks worn by certain European judges.
American justices since at least the time of John Marshall have eschewed such fin-
ery (wearing plain black robes), so this reference is clearly meant not as a factual
description of the justices' attire, but rather as a critique of the elitist nature of the
judiciary as an institution.
[3] The reference here is likely to the fact that agriculture no longer dominated European economies and had been far eclipsed by manufacturing.

industry.[4] A vast conspiracy against mankind has been organized on two continents, and it is rapidly taking possession of the world. If not met and overthrown at once it forebodes terrible social convulsions, the destruction of civilization, or the establishment of an absolute despotism.

We have witnessed for more than a quarter of a century the struggles of the two great political parties for power and plunder, while grievous wrongs have been inflicted upon the suffering people. We charge that the controlling influences dominating both these parties have permitted the existing dreadful conditions to develop without serious effort to prevent or restrain them. Neither do they now promise us any substantial reform. They have agreed together to ignore, in the coming campaign, every issue but one. They propose to drown the outcries of a plundered people with the uproar of a sham battle over the tariff, so that capitalists, corporations, national banks, rings, trusts, watered stock, the demonetization of silver and the oppressions of the usurers may all be lost sight of. They propose to sacrifice our homes, lives, and children on the altar of mammon;[5] to destroy the multitude in order to secure corruption funds from the millionaires.

Assembled on the anniversary of the birthday of the nation, and filled with the spirit of the grand general and chief who established our independence, we seek to restore the government of the Republic to the hands of "the plain people," with which class it originated. We assert our purposes to be identical with the purposes of the National Constitution; to form a more perfect union and establish justice, insure domestic tranquility, provide for the common defence, promote the general welfare, and secure the blessings of liberty for ourselves and our posterity.

We declare that this Republic can only endure as a free government while built upon the love of the whole people for each other and for the nation; that it cannot be pinned together by bayonets; that the Civil War is over, and that every passion and resentment which grew out of it must die with it, and that we must be in fact, as we are in name, one united brotherhood of free men.

Our country finds itself confronted by conditions for which there is no

---

[4] This is the influence of what the Populists referred to as the "money power" that took the form of Eastern banks and industrial monopolies. These groups financed farmers' mortgages, determined the rates railroads charged to carry their produce to market, and then played a major role in setting the prices for their products. When times were good, the money power took an unfair share of farmers' profits; when times were bad, the money power took farmers' homes.

[5] The name of the devil of greed in Milton; more generally, a reference to wealth regarded as an evil influence or as an idol.

precedent in the history of the world; our annual agricultural productions amount to billions of dollars in value, which must, within a few weeks or months, be exchanged for billions of dollars' worth of commodities consumed in their production; the existing currency supply is wholly inadequate to make this exchange; the results are falling prices, the formation of combines and rings, the impoverishment of the producing class. We pledge ourselves that if given power we will labor to correct these evils by wise and reasonable legislation, in accordance with the terms of our platform.

We believe that the power of government—in other words, of the people—should be expanded (as in the case of the postal service) as rapidly and as far as the good sense of an intelligent people and the teachings of experience shall justify, to the end that oppression, injustice, and poverty shall eventually cease in the land.

While our sympathies as a party of reform are naturally upon the side of every proposition which will tend to make men intelligent, virtuous, and temperate, we nevertheless regard these questions, important as they are, as secondary to the great issues now pressing for solution, and upon which not only our individual prosperity but the very existence of free institutions depend; and we ask all men to first help us to determine whether we are to have a republic to administer before we differ as to the conditions upon which it is to be administered, believing that the forces of reform this day organized will never cease to move forward until every wrong is remedied and equal rights and equal privileges securely established for all the men and women of this country.

PLATFORM.

We declare, therefore—

First.—That the union of the labor forces of the United States this day consummated shall be permanent and perpetual; may its spirit enter into all hearts for the salvation of the Republic and the uplifting of mankind.

Second.—Wealth belongs to him who creates it, and every dollar taken from industry without an equivalent is robbery. "If any will not work, neither shall he eat."[6] The interest of rural and civic[7] labor are the same; their enemies are identical.

---

[6] This quote, from the Bible, is attributed to Paul the Apostle (II Thessalonians 3:10).
[7] Industrial.

Third.—We believe that the time has come when the railroad corporations will either own the people or the people must own the railroads, and should the government enter upon the work of owning and managing all railroads, we should favor an amendment to the Constitution by which all persons engaged in the government service shall be placed under a civil-service regulation of the most rigid character, so as to prevent the increase of the power of the national administration by the use of such additional government employees.

Finance.—We demand a national currency, safe, sound, and flexible, issued by the general government only, a full legal tender for all debts, public and private, and that without the use of banking corporations, a just, equitable, and efficient means of distribution direct to the people, at a tax not to exceed 2 per cent. per annum, to be provided as set forth in the sub-treasury plan of the Farmers' Alliance,[8] or a better system; also by payments in discharge of its obligations for public improvements.

We demand free and unlimited coinage of silver and gold at the present legal ratio of 16 to 1.

We demand that the amount of circulating medium be speedily increased to not less than $50 per capita.

We demand a graduated income tax.

We believe that the money of the country should be kept as much as possible in the hands of the people, and hence we demand that all State and national revenues shall be limited to the necessary expenses of the government, economically and honestly administered.

We demand that postal savings banks be established by the government for the safe deposit of the earnings of the people and to facilitate exchange.

Transportation.—Transportation being a means of exchange and a public necessity, the government should own and operate the railroads in the interest of the people. The telegraph, telephone, like the post-office system, being a necessity for the transmission of news, should be owned and operated by the government in the interest of the people.

Land.—The land, including all the natural sources of wealth, is the heritage of the people, and should not be monopolized for speculative purposes,

---

[8] Farmers' Alliances were the early incarnation of the Populists. First organized in Texas in 1878, they became conduits for early political action to address later Populist concerns.

and alien ownership of land[9] should be prohibited. All land now held by railroads and other corporations in excess of their actual needs, and all lands
now owned by aliens should be reclaimed by the government and held for
actual settlers only.

---

[9] An alien is a foreign national.

The "Cross of Gold" Speech

William Jennings Bryan

July 9, 1896

A t the Democratic National Convention in 1896, proponents of "free silver" (the re-legalization of silver as part of the nation's monetary standards) appeared to possess the two-thirds majority needed to nominate a candidate. Unfortunately, they did not have a candidate. There was no doubt the platform would endorse the unlimited coinage of silver, but a candidate was needed who could sell the position to the American people. On the night of July 8, William Jennings Bryan revealed himself as the candidate the silverites were looking for by delivering one of the most famous speeches in American history. At the time, Bryan was a former member of Congress from Nebraska who had been working tirelessly to build support for his candidacy. His passionate speech electrified the crowd and convinced the members of the convention to nominate him as their candidate on the fifth ballot. Bryan then ran a whistle-stop campaign (a train tour bringing his message to the people), traveling around the country giving hundreds of speeches before finally losing to Republican William McKinley.

SOURCE: *Official Proceedings of the Democratic National Convention Held in Chicago, Illinois, July 7–11, 1896* (Logansport, Ind., 1896), 226–234.

Mr. BRYAN: Mr. Chairman and Gentleman of the Convention: I would be presumptuous, indeed, to present myself against the distinguished gentlemen to whom you have listened if this were but a measuring of ability; but this is not a contest among persons. "The humblest citizen in all the land, when clad in armor of a righteous cause, is stronger than all the whole hosts of error that they can bring." I come to speak to you in defense of a cause as holy as the cause of liberty—the cause of humanity. When this debate is concluded a motion will be made to lay upon the table the resolution offered in commendation of the administration and also the resolution in condemnation of the Administration. I shall object to bringing this question down to a level of persons. The individual is but an atom; he is born, he acts, he dies but principles are eternal; and this has been a contest of principle.

Never before in the history of this country has there been witnessed such a contest as that through which we have passed. Never before in the history of American politics has a great issue been fought out, as this issue has been, by the voters themselves.

On the 4th of March, 1895, a few Democrats, most of them members of Congress, issued an address to the Democrats of the nation asserting that the money question was the paramount issue of the hour; asserting also the right of a majority of the Democratic party to control the position of the party on this paramount issue; concluding with the request that all believers in free coinage of silver in the Democratic party should organize and take charge of and control the policy of the Democratic party. Three months later, at Memphis, an organization was perfected, and the silver Democrats went forth openly and boldly and courageously proclaiming their belief and declaring that if successful they would crystallize in a platform the declaration what they had made; and then began the conflict with a zeal approaching the zeal which inspired the crusaders who followed PETER the Hermit.[1] Our silver Democrats went forth from victory unto victory until they are assembled now, not to discuss, not to debate, but to enter up the judgment rendered by the plain people of this country.

...We come to speak for this broader class of business men. Ah, my friends, we say not one word against those who live upon the Atlantic coast; but those hardy pioneers who braved all the dangers of the wilderness, who have made the desert to blossom as the rose—those pioneers away out there, rearing their children near to nature's heart, where they can mingle their voices with the voices of the birds—out there where they have erected school houses for the education of their children and churches where they praise their Creator, and the cemeteries where sleep the ashes of their dead—are as deserving of the consideration of this party as any people in this country.

It is for these that we speak. We do not come us aggressors. Our war is not a war of conquest. We are fighting in the defense of our homes, our families and posterity. We have petitioned, and our petitions have been scorned. We have entreated and our entreaties have been disregard. We have begged, and they have mocked when our calamity came.

---

[1] Considered one of the most important preachers of the First Crusade.

We beg no longer; we entreat no more; we petition no more. We defy them!

... The income tax is a just law. It simply intends to put the burdens of government justly upon the backs of the people. I am in favor of an income tax. When I find a man who is not willing to pay his share of the burden of the government which protects him I find a man who is unworthy to enjoy the blessings of a government like ours.

... Mr. JEFFERSON,[2] who was once regarded as good Democratic authority, seems to have a different opinion from the gentleman who has addressed us on the part of the minority. Those who are opposed to this proposition tell us that the issue of paper money is a function of the bank, and that the Government ought to go out of the banking business. I stand with JEFFERSON, rather than with them, and tell them, as he did, that the issue of money is a function of the Government, and that the banks should go out of the governing business.

They complain about the plank which declares against the life tenure in office. They have tried to strain it to mean that which it does not mean. What we oppose in that plank is the life tenure that is being built up in Washington which establishes an office-holding class and excludes from participation in the benefits the humbler members of our society. I cannot dwell longer in my limited time upon these things.

... Now, my friends, let me come to the great paramount issue. If they ask us here why it is we say more on the money question than we say upon the tariff question, I reply that if protection has slain its thousands the gold standard has slain its tens of thousands. If they ask us why we did not embody all these things in our platform which we believe, we reply to them that when we have restored the money of the constitution all other necessary reforms will be possible, and that until that is done there is no reforms will be possible, and that until that is done there is no reform that can be accomplished.

... Why this change? Ah, my friends, is not the change evident to anyone who will look at the matter? It is because no private character, however pure, no personal popularity, however great, can protect from the avenging wrath of an indignant people the man who will either declare that he is in favor of fastening the gold standard upon this people, or who is willing to surrender

---

[2] Thomas Jefferson (1743–1826), author of the Declaration of Independence, who later served as vice president under John Adams and then as president from 1801 to 1809.

the right of self-government and place legislative control in the hands of foreign potentates and powers.

We go forth confident that we shall win. Why? Because upon the paramount issue in this campaign there is not a spot of ground upon which the enemy will dare to challenge battle. Why, if they tell us that the gold standard is a good thing, we point to their platform and tell them that their platform pledges the party to get rid of a gold standard, and substitute bimetallism. If the gold standard is a good thing why try to get rid of it? If the gold standard, and I might call your attention to the fact that some of the very people who are in this convention to-day and who tell you that we ought to declare in favor of international bimetallism and thereby declare that the gold standard is wrong, and that the principles of bimetallism are better—these very people four months ago were open and avowed advocates of the gold standard and telling us that we could not legislate two metals together even with all the world.

I want to suggest this truth, that if the gold standard is a good thing we ought to declare in favor its retention and not in favor of abandoning it; and if the gold standard is a bad thing why should we wait until some other nations are willing to help us to let it go?

Here is the line of battle. We care not upon which issue they force the fight. We are prepared to meet them on either issue or on both. If they tell us that the gold standard is the standard of civilization we reply to them that this, the most enlightened of all nations of the earth, has never declared for a gold standard, and both the parties this year are declaring against it. If the gold standard is the standard of civilization, why, my friends, should we not have it? So if they come to meet us on that we can present the history of our nation. More than that. We can tell them this, that they will search the pages of history in vain to find a single instance in which the common people of any land ever declared themselves in favor of a gold standard. They can find where the holders of fixed investments have.

... There are two ideas of government. There are those who believe that if you just legislate to make the well-to-do prosperous that their prosperity will leak through on those below. The Democratic idea has been that if you legislate to make the masses prosperous their prosperity will find its way up and through every class that rests upon it.

You come to use and tell us that the great cities are in favor of the gold standard. I tell you that the great cities rest upon these broad and fertile prairies. Burn down your cities and leave our farms, and your cities will spring up again as if by magic. But destroy our farms and the grass will grow in the streets of every city in this country.

My friends, we shall declare that this nation is able to legislate for its own people on every question, without waiting for the aid or consent of any other nation on earth, and upon that issue we expect to carry every single State in this Union.

...If they dare to come out and in the open defend the gold standard as a good thing, we shall fight them to the uttermost, having behind us the producing masses of the Nation and the world. Having behind us the commercial interests and the laboring interests and all the toiling masses, we shall answer their demands for a gold standard by saying to them, you shall not press down upon the brow of labor this crown of thorns. You shall not crucify mankind upon a cross of gold.

"Peril in the Machine"

Robert La Follette

February 23, 1897

T*hroughout most of the nineteenth century, national conventions selected the presidential nominees of each party. In earlier times, these conventions were highly participatory and did a fairly accurate job of gauging voter intentions. Over time, however, these conventions fell increasingly under the power of political bosses (individuals who control various parts of a political party, such as a ward or precinct) who controlled the selection of delegates to the state party conventions and thereby indirectly decided the delegates to the national conventions. The selection of party nominees thus lost its democratic character and became a function of party elites doing the selecting in the proverbial smoke-filled rooms.*

Robert La Follette was the leader of a group of progressive reformers who led an attack on the power of state and national conventions. La Follette and others advocated the use of primaries instead of conventions as a way to carry out the task of nomination. Primaries were popular elections that would replace the conventions in nominating candidates for office. They had the advantage of removing control over the conventions from party leaders and giving the public a real voice in the nominating process. In 1912, La Follette challenged incumbent president Howard Taft for the Republican nomination in the first presidential election to use primaries.

SOURCE: Robert La Follette, "Peril in the Machine," *Chicago Times-Herald*, February 23, 1897. https://www.wisconsinhistory.org/Records/Newspaper/BA1995.

In every democracy men will affiliate with one or the other of two great political parties. The ballot must determine which party shall administer government, enact new legislation, adjust the laws to all the complex social relations of life, to all the complicated business transactions of millions of human beings with order and justice. The ballot can achieve the kind of administration desired, establish the economic and financial policies essential, only through the election of men of integrity and ability, embodying the ideas expressed in the ballot. That the voter may be thoroughly informed upon the questions involved and upon the men to be chosen as the representatives of his convictions there should be the widest discussion and the most searching investigation.

The fundamental principle of a republic is individual responsibility. The responsibility is personal at the point in our political system where the citizen comes in direct contact with the system itself. This is the initial point of all legislation, all administration. In all the activities preliminary to the primary, and in the primary itself, the citizen is an elementary force in government. Here the voter can lay his hand directly upon the shoulder of the public servant and point the way he should go. But this ends with the adjournment of the primary or caucus. From that moment the citizen in a representative democracy, under a caucus, delegate and convention system, does not again come in direct personal touch with the work either of legislation or administration. How essential, then, if he is to be a factor in government, that he take part, and intelligently, too, in this fundamental work. If there be failure here, there is failure throughout . . . .

Remedy Is Suggested

What, then, shall we do to be saved?

Waste no more time in vain sermons on the duty of attending the caucus. It is too late for that. Except at long intervals, when in a sort of frenzy the citizen strikes at the machine shackles, men can be no longer drafted into caucus attendance. They have seen the game before. They know the dice are loaded. They are no longer indifferent to their duties, nor ignorant of the situation. They well understand that their only part in government is to vote the ticket prepared for them and bear the machine rule of their own party, or the machine rule of the other party. They know they do not get the kind of government they vote for, but they do the best they can. They still attend the elections. They are as vitally interested in good government as ever. They are only waiting to find the way to achieve it. Here is our final safety. Here is the ultimate overthrow of the machine. If we provide the same safeguards, the same certainty, the same facility for expressing and executing the will of the people at the primaries as now prevail at the elections, we shall have the same general interest, the same general participation in the one as in the other.

Aye, more than this, if we guarantee the American citizen a full voice in the selection of candidates, and shaping the policy of his party and the administration of government incident thereto, then shall we invest not only the primaries, but the elections as well, with an abiding interest for him, extending beyond the day of the primaries and the day of the election, the weeks of the campaign—indeed, we shall make the primary and the election of vastly deeper significance, appealing in a new way to his deliberate judgment, his patriotism and his personal responsibility.

It is as much the interest and as plainly the duty of the state to as carefully perfect and guard a system of nominating candidates as it perfects and guards the system of electing them.

The caucus, delegate and convention system is inherently bad. It invites to manipulation, scheming, trickery, corruption and fraud. Even if the caucus were fairly conducted, the plan of which it is a part removes the nomination too far from the voter. Every transfer of delegated power weakens responsibility, until finally, by the time it is lodged in the hands of a nominating convention, the sense of responsibility has been lost in transit, unless it has been ticketed through by instructions from its original source. And even then all along the journey, from the primary to the convention, the confidential agents of the machine are introducing delegates to the mysteries of "gold brick" and "three card" political schemes.[1]

The convention under the most favorable conditions is anything but a deliberative body. Its work is hurried and business necessarily transacted in confusion. There is great excitement. It is the storm center of a political tempest. There are rumors and roorbacks, challenges and dentals. There is no time for investigation and no opportunity to distinguish the real issue from the false issue. Charges are withheld and "sprung" in the convention purposely to avoid disproval and mislead delegates; and the dark horse is ever in reserve, waiting a favorable opportunity to take the convention unawares. Add to this all the corruption which comes with machine domination of a convention and you have political disaster and political crime as a result.

If, after long suffering and misrepresentation, the people by tremendous and united effort could succeed in defeating and even destroying the machine, the opportunity offered by the caucus and convention plan would simply restore the old or build up a new machine in its place.

---

[1] Gold brick schemes involve selling a tangible item for more than it is worth. They are named after a scam in which a buyer pays for a golden ingot which turns out to be gold-plated lead. Three card schemes, also known as three-card monte, involve tricking the victim into betting that they can find the "money" card among three face-down playing cards.

Drop Caucus and Convention.

No, no! Beginning the work in the state, put aside the caucus and the convention. They have been and will continue to be prostituted to the service of corrupt organization. They answer no purpose further than to give respectable form to political robbery. Abolish the caucus and the convention. Go back to the first principles of democracy. Go back to the people. Substitute for the caucus and the convention a primary election—held under all the sanctions of law which prevail at the general elections—where the citizen may cast his vote directly to nominate the candidate of the party with which he affiliates and have it canvasses and returned just as he cast it.

Provide a means of placing the candidates in nomination before the primary and forestall the creation of a new caucus system back of the primary election.

Provide a ballet for the primary election and print on it the names of all candidates for nomination who have previously filed preliminary nomination papers with a designated official.

Provide that no candidate for nomination shall be entitled to have his name printed on the primary election ticket who shall not have been called out as a candidate by the written request of a given percentage if the vote cast at the preceding election in the district, county or state in which he is proposed as a candidate in the same manner that judicial candidates are now called out in many states.

Provide for the selection of a committee to represent the party organization and promulgate the party platform by the election at the primary of a representative man from the party for each county in the state.

Under severe penalty for violation of the law prohibit electioneering in or about the election booth, punish bribery and the singular attempt to bribe and protect fully the counting and return of the votes cast.

Do this and the knell of the political machine has sounded in the state.

Then every citizen will share equally in the nomination of the candidates of his party and attend primary election as a privilege as well as a duty. It will no longer be necessary to create an artificial interest in the general election to induce voters to attend. Intelligent, well-considered judgment will be substituted for unthinking enthusiasm; the lamp of reason for the torchlight.

The voter will not have to be persuaded that he has an interest in the election; he will know that he has. The nominations of the party will not be the result of "compromise" or impulse or evil design—the barrel or the machine—but the candidates of the majority honestly and fairly nominated.

To every generation some important work is committed. If this generation will destroy the political machine, will emancipate the majority from its enslavement, will [a]gain place the destinies of this nation in the [ha]nds of its citizens, then, "under God this government of the people by the people and for the [peop]le shall not perish from the earth."[22]

---

[2] Abraham Lincoln's Gettysburg Address.

Plunkitt of Tammany Hall

George Washington Plunkitt

1905

G eorge Washington Plunkitt was born into poverty and received only three
years of formal education, but this did not stop him from rising in the ranks
of Tammany Hall, the New York Democratic political machine. A political
machine, as opposed to the political party, was a party organization headed by
a single boss or small group that held enough votes to maintain political and
administrative control of a city, county, or state. Often these machines provided
goods and social services that struggling local governments were unable to give
to the people. William "Boss" Tweed, head of Tammany Hall, for example, was
able to build a loyal following by performing favors for immigrant groups, such
as providing jobs or securing housing.

Plunkitt served as state senator and a representative to the New York Assembly, but was best known and most influential acting as a ward boss (that is, a local
political party organizer) in New York's Fifteenth Assembly District. Plunkitt
built a substantial and powerful following among the working-class Irish of the
district by doing political favors and providing services for the people. At the same
time, he became independently wealthy by manipulating the political system and
trading political favors for insider information. These practices, which Plunkitt
candidly (if ironically) defended as "honest graft," provide a close-up look at the
functioning and practices of the big city machines. Plunkitt was only too happy to
defend these practices against accusations of corruption and inefficiency.

SOURCE: William Riordan, *Plunkitt of Tammany Hall: A Series of Very Plain Talks on Very
Practical Politics* (New York: McClure, Philips, 1905), 3–16. https://archive.org/details/
plunkittoftammanoorior/page/n9.

Chapter 1: Honest Graft and Dishonest Graft

EVERYBODY is talkin' these days about Tammany men growin' rich on graft, but nobody thinks of drawin' the distinction between honest graft and dishonest graft. There's all the difference in the world between the two. Yes, many of our men have grown rich in politics. I have myself. I've made a big fortune out of the game, and I'm gettin' richer every day, but I've not gone in for dishonest graft—blackmailin' gamblers, saloonkeepers, disorderly people, etc.—and neither has any of the men who have made big fortunes in politics.

There's an honest graft, and I'm an example of how it works. I might sum up the whole thing by sayin': I seen my opportunities and I took 'em.

Just let me explain by examples. My party's in power in the city, and it's goin' to undertake a lot of public improvements. Well, I'm tipped off, say, that they're going to lay out a new park at a certain place.

I see my opportunity and I take it. I go to that place and I buy up all the land I can in the neighborhood. The the board of this or that makes its plan public, and there is a rush to get my land, which nobody cared particular for before.

Ain't it perfectly honest to charge a good price and make a profit on my investment and foresight? Of course, it is. Well, that's honest graft.

Or, supposin' it's a new bridge they're goin' to build. I get tipped off and I buy as much property as I can that has to be taken for approaches. I sell at my own price later on and drop some more money in the bank.

Wouldn't you? It's just lookin' ahead in Wall Street or in the coffee or cotton market. It's honest graft, and I'm lookin' for it every day in the year. I will tell you frankly that I've got a good lot of it, too.

I'll tell you of one case. They were goin' to fix up a bid park, no matter where. I got on to it, and went lookin' about for land in that neighborhood.

I could get nothin' at a bargain but a big piece of swamp, but I took it fast enough and held on to it. What turned out was just what I counted on. They couldn't make the park complete without Plunkitt's swamp, and they had to pay a good price for it. Anything dishonest in that?

Up in the watershed I made some money, too. I bought up several bits of land there some years ago and made a pretty good guess that they would be bought up for water purposes later by the city.

Somehow, I always guessed about right, and shouldn't I enjoy the profit of my foresight? It was rather amusin' when the condemnation commissioners came along and found piece after piece of the land in the name of George

Plunkitt of the Fifteenth Assembly District, New York City. They wondered how I knew just what to buy. The answer is—I seen my opportunity and I took it. I haven't confined myself to land; anything that pays is in my line.

For instance, the city is repavin' a street and has several hundred thousand old granite blocks to sell. I am on hand to buy, and I know just what they are worth.

How? Never mind that. I had a sort of monopoly of this business for a while, but once a newspaper tried to do me. It got some outside men to come over from Brooklyn and New Jersey to bid against me.

Was I done? Not much. I went to each of the men and said: "How many of these 250,000 stories do you want?" One said 20,000, and another wanted 15,000, and other wanted 10,000. I said: "All right, let me bid for the lot, and I'll give each of you all you want for nothin'".

They agreed, of course. Then the auctioneer yelled: "How much am I bid for these 250,000 fine pavin' stones?"

"Two dollars and fifty cents," says I.

"Two dollars and fifty cents!" screamed the auctioneer. "Oh, that's a joke! Give me a real bid."

He found the bid was real enough. My rivals stood silent. I got the lot for $2.50 and gave them their share. That's how the attempt to do Plunkitt ended, and that's how all such attempts end.

I've told you how I got rich by honest graft. Now, let me tell you that most politicians who are accused of robbin' the city get rich the same way.

They didn't steal a dollar from the city treasury. They just seen their opportunities and took them. That is why, when a reform administration comes in and spends a half million dollars in tryin' to find the public robberies they talked about in the campaign, they don't find them.

The books are always all right. The money in the city treasury is all right. Everything is all right. All they can show is that the Tammany heads of departments looked after their friends, within the law, and gave them what opportunities they could to make honest graft. Now, let me tell you that's never goin' to hurt Tammany with the people. Every good man looks after his friends, and any man who doesn't isn't likely to be popular. If I have a good thing to hand out in private life, I give it to a friend—Why shouldn't I do the same in public life?

Another kind of honest graft. Tammany has raised a good many salaries. There was an awful howl by the reformers, but don't you know that Tammany gains ten votes for every one it lost by salary raisin'?

The Wall Street banker thinks it shameful to raise a department clerk's salary from $1500 to $1800 a year, but every man who draws a salary himself says: "That's all right. I wish it was me." And he feels very much like votin' the Tammany[1] ticket on election day, just out of sympathy.

Tammany was beat in 1901 because the people were deceived into believin' that it worked dishonest graft. They didn't draw a distinction between dishonest and honest graft, but they saw that some Tammany men grew rich, and supposed they had been robbin' the city treasury or levyin' blackmail on disorderly houses, or workin' in with the gamblers and lawbreakers.

As a matter of policy, if nothing else, why should the Tammany leaders go into such dirty business, when there is so much honest graft lyin' around when they are in power? Did you ever consider that?

Now, in conclusion, I want to say that I don't own a dishonest dollar. If my worst enemy was given the job of writin' my epitaph when I'm gone, he couldn't do more than write:

"George W. Plunkitt. He Seen His Opportunities, and He Took 'Em."

Chapter 2: How to Become a Statesman

THERE'S thousands of young men in this city who will go to the polls for the first time next November. Among them will be many who have watched the careers of successful men in politics, and who are longin' to make names and fortunes for themselves at the same game—It is to these youths that I want to give advice. First, let me say that I am in a position to give what the courts call expert testimony on the subject. I don't think you can easily find a better example than I am of success in politics. After forty years' experience at the game I am—well, I'm George Washington Plunkitt. Everybody knows what figure I cut in the greatest organization on earth, and if you hear people say that I've laid away a million or so since I was a butcher's boy in Washington Market, don't come to me for an indignant denial. I'm pretty comfortable, thank you.

...Another mistake: some young men think that the best way to prepare for the political game is to practice speakin' and becomin' orators. That's all wrong. We've got some orators in Tammany Hall, but they're chiefly ornamental. You never heard of Charlie Murphy[2] delivering a speech, did you? Or

---

[1] Tammany Hall was the Democratic political machine that controlled New York City and New York State politics through most of the nineteenth century.
[2] Known as Silent Charlie Murphy, he was a political boss of Tammany Hall and was responsible for raising it to a level of respectability.

Richard Croker,[3] or John Kelly,[4] or any other man who has been a real power in the organization? Look at the thirty-six district leaders of Tammany Hall today. How many of them travel on their tongues? Maybe one or two, and they don't count when business is doin' at Tammany Hall. The men who rule have practiced keepin' their tongues still, not exercisin' them. So you want to drop the orator idea unless you mean to go into politics just to perform the sky-rocket act.

... That was beginnin' business in a small way, wasn't it? But that is the only way to become a real lastin' statesman. I soon branched out. Two young men in the flat next to mine were school friends—I went to them, just as I went to Tommy, and they agreed to stand by me. Then I had a followin' of three voters and I began to get a bit chesty. Whenever I dropped into district head-quarters, everybody shook hands with me, and the leader one day honored me by lightin' a match for my cigar. And so it went on like a snowball rollin' down a hill I worked the flat-house that I lived in from the basement to the top floor, and I got about a dozen young men to follow me. Then I tackled the next house and so on down the block and around the corner. Before long I had sixty men back of me and formed the George Washington Plunkitt Association....

---

[3] Known as Boss Croker, he was an Irish American politician who led Tammany Hall as a political boss.
[4] Known as Honest John, he was a boss of Tammany Hall and a US Representative from New York from 1855 to 1858.

DOCUMENT 21

"Party Government in the United States"

Woodrow Wilson

1908

W ilson wrote that the party system of the nineteenth century was untenable. Unelected and therefore unaccountable party bosses could no longer be permitted to control public officials. Parties needed to serve the will of the people and, once free of the party bosses, could be made more accountable to public opinion. Wilson also complained in his writings that American political parties suffered from a lack of strong internal organization and discipline. Rank-and-file party members frequently dissented from party leadership with no repercussions or penalties. This meant that parties were not held accountable to the party platform and by extension were not held accountable to public opinion. This was true even of the Speaker of the House, who was regularly held in check by the standing House committees.

In place of this arrangement, Wilson wanted a truly accountable party system. Parties aid in making the connection more immediate between the people and their governing institutions. Party members in the legislature, he argued, should be clearly organized and guided by leaders that are easily recognizable by the public. This would allow voters to accept or reject leaders as a way of making their will known on policy matters. This would keep members of Congress accountable to the people by reminding party members that the public was always watching and would hold responsible parties that failed to live up to voters' expectations.

SOURCE: Woodrow Wilson, "Party Government in the United States," in *Constitutional Government in the United States* (New York: Columbia University Press, 1917), 198–222.

CHAPTER 8. PARTY GOVERNMENT
IN THE UNITED STATES

[Wilson begins the chapter with an extended history of Whig theory in England.]

...Just because, therefore, there is nowhere else in the world so complex and various an electoral machinery as in the United States, nowhere else in the world is party machinery so elaborate or so necessary. It is important to keep this in mind. Otherwise, when we analyze party action, we shall fall into the too common error of thinking that we are analyzing disease. As a matter of fact, the whole thing is just as normal and natural as any other political development. The part that party has played in this country has been both necessary and beneficial, and if bosses and secret managers are often undesirable persons, playing their parts for their own benefit or glorification rather than for the public good, they are at least the natural fruits of the tree. It has borne fruit good and bad, sweet and bitter, wholesome and corrupt, but it is native to our air and practice and can be uprooted only by an entire change of system.

All the peculiarities of party government in the United States are due to the too literal application of Whig[1] doctrine, to the infinite multiplication of elective offices. There are two things to be done for which we have supplied no adequate legal or constitutional machinery: there are thousands of officials to be chosen and there are many disconnected parts of government to be brought into cooperation. "It may be laid down as a political maxim that whatever assigns to the people a power which they are naturally incapable of wielding takes it away from them." They have, under our Constitution and statutes, been assigned the power of filling innumerable elective offices; they are incapable of wielding that power because they have neither the time nor the necessary means of cooperative action; the power has therefore been taken away from them, not by law but by circumstances, and handed over to those who have the time and the inclination to supply the necessary organization; and the system of election has been transformed into a system of practically irresponsible appointment to office by private party managers,—irresponsible because our law has not yet been able to devise any means of making it responsible. It may also be laid down as a political maxim that when the several chief organs of government are separated by organic law and offset against each other in jealous seclusion, no common legal authority set over them, no necessary community of interest subsisting amongst them, no common origin or purpose dominating them, they must of necessity, if united at all, be united by pressure from without; and they must be united if government is to proceed. They cannot remain checked and balanced against

---

[1] A member of the British parliament constitutional party that sought the supremacy of Parliament in government.

one another; they must act, and act together. They must, therefore, of their own will or of mere necessity obey an outside master.

... It is interesting to observe that as a consequence the distinction we make between "politicians" and "statesmen" is peculiarly our own. In other countries where these words or their equivalents are used, the statesman differs from the politician only in capacity and in degree, and is distinguished as a public leader only in being a greater figure on the same stage, whereas with us politicians and statesmen differ in kind. A politician is a man who manages the organs of the party outside the open field of government, outside executive offices and legislative chambers, and who conveys the behests of party to those who hold the offices and make laws; while the statesman is the leader of public opinion, the immediate director (under the politicians) of executive or legislative policy, the diplomat, the recognized public servant. The politician, indeed, often hold public office and attempts the role of statesman as well, but, though the roles may be combined, they are none the less sharply distinguishable. Party majorities which are actually in control of the whole legislative machinery, as party majorities in England are, determine party programs by the use of the government itself,—politicians, I mean who are, at any rate in respect of that function, independent of the responsibilities of office and of public action; and these independent conventions, not charged with the responsibility of carrying out their programs, actually outline the policy of administrations and dictate the action of Congress, the irresponsible dictating to the responsible, and so, it may be, destroying the very responsibility itself. "The peculiarities of American party government are all due to this separation of party management from direct and immediate responsibility for the administration of the government."

... The machinery of party rule is nominally representative. The several assemblies and conventions through which the parties operate are supposed to be made up of delegates chosen by the voters of the party, to speak for them with a certain knowledge of what they want and expect. But here again the action of the voters themselves is hardly more than nominal. The lists of delegates are made up by the party managers as freely in all ordinary circumstances as are the lists of the candidates in whose selection they concur. To add the duty of really selecting delegates to the duty of selecting men for office already laid upon our voters by law would be only to add to the impossibility of their task, and to their confusion if they attempted to perform it. When difficulties arise in the process, rival bodies of delegates can always be chosen, and then the managing committees who are in charge of the party's affairs—the county committee, the state committee, or the national committee—can dictate which of the contesting delegations shall be admitted, which shall have their credentials accepted. It is to this necessity we have been brought by farming the functions of government out to outside parties. We have made the task of the voter hopeless and therefore impossible.

And yet at the best the control which party exercises over government is uncertain. There can be, whether for the voter or for the managing politician himself, little more than a presumption that what party managers propose and promise will be done, for the separation of authority between the several organs of government itself still stands in the way. Government is still in solution, and nothing may come to crystallization. But we may congratulate ourselves that we have succeeded as well as we have in giving our politics unity and coherence. We should have drifted sadly, should much oftener have been made to guess what the course of our politics should be, had we not constructed this singular and, on the whole, efficient machinery by which we have in all ordinary seasons contrived to hold the *personnel* and the policy of our government together.

... It is in this vital sense that our national parties have been our veritable body politic. The very compulsion of selfishness has made them serviceable; the very play of self-interest has made them effective. In organization was their strength. It brought them the rewards of local office, the command of patronage of many kinds, the detailed control of opinion, the subtle mastery of every force of growth and expansion. They strove for nothing so constantly or so watchfully as for the compact, cooperative organization and action which served to hold the nation in their hands.

But we have come within sight of the end of the merely nationalizing process. Contrasts between region and region become every year less obvious, conflicts of interest less acute and disturbing. Party organization is no longer needed for the mere rudimentary task of holding the machinery together or giving it the sustenance of some common object, some single cooperative motive. The time is at hand when we can with safety examine the network of party in its detail and change its structure without imperiling its strength. This thing that has served us so well might now master us if we left it irresponsible. We must see to it that it is made responsible.

I have already explained in what sense and for what very sufficient reasons it is irresponsible. Party organizations appoint our elective officers, and we do not elect them. The chief obstacle to their reform, the chief thing that has stood in the way of making them amenable to opinion, controllable by independent opposition, is the reverence with which we have come to regard them. By binding us together at moments of crisis they have won our affectionate fealty. Because the Republican party "saved the Union," a whole generation went by, in many parts of the country, before men who had acted with it in a time of crisis could believe it possible for any "gentleman" or patriot to break away from it or oppose it, whatever its policy and however remote from anything it had originally professed or undertaken. Because the Democratic party had stood for state rights and a power freely dispersed among the people, because it had tried to avoid war and preserve the old harmony of the sections, men of the same fervor of sympathy in other parts of the country deemed it equally incredible that any man of breeding or of principle could turn his back upon it or act with any other political organization. The feeling lasted until lines of party division became equally fixed and artificial. But with changing generations feelings change. We are coming now to look upon our parties once more as instruments for progressive action, as means for handling the affairs of a new age. Sentimental reminiscences is less dominant over us. We are ready to study new uses for our parties and to adapt them to new standards and principles.

The principle of change, if change there is to be, should spring out of this question: Have we had enough of the literal translation of Whig theory into practice, into constitutions? Are we ready to make our legislatures and our executives our real bodies politic, instead of our parties? If we are, we must think less of checks and balances and more of coordinated power, less of separation of functions and more of the synthesis of action. If we are, we must decrease the number and complexity of the things the voter is called upon to do; concentrate his attention upon a few men whom he can make responsible, a few objects upon which he can easily centre his purpose; make parties his instruments and not his masters by an utter simplification of the things he is expected to look to.

"The New Nationalism"

Theodore Roosevelt

September 1, 1910

*T*he themes of Roosevelt's speech would form the foundation of his 1912 presidential campaign representing the Bull Moose Party. The speech includes an
admission from Roosevelt that his progressive policy goals would require a massive
increase in the size of government as well as significant intrusions into the private
sphere. Delivered in Kansas at Osawatomie in front of 30,000 listeners, the supposed occasion for the speech was the dedicatory ceremonies at the John Brown
Memorial Park. The park commemorated the skirmish between proslavery forces
and the men led by Brown during the "Battle of Osawatomie." Response to the
speech was mixed, with some calling it communistic, socialistic, or anarchistic,
while others hailed the speech as one of the greatest ever given in America.

Roosevelt worried about the power of the minority—often politicians—over the
majority and advocated changes that would make government more accountable
to the people. These included the initiative, referendum, recall, and direct election of US senators. Roosevelt also wanted more accountable parties that would
respond to popular desires and needs. He believed the political bosses wielded too
much power and that parties needed to unite behind strong leadership, which he
was happy to provide from the presidency. To that end, Roosevelt favored direct
primaries as a means of nominating candidates for office, believing that they
would give candidates a broad base of popular support and hold them accountable to the people.

SOURCE: Theodore Roosevelt, *The New Nationalism* (New York: Outlook Company, 1910),
3–33.

. . . Nothing is more true than that excess of every kind is followed by reaction; a fact which should be pondered by reformer and reactionary alike.
We are face to face with new conceptions of the relations of property to
human welfare, chiefly because certain advocates of the rights of property
as against the rights of men have been pushing their claims too far. The man

who wrongly holds that every human right is secondary to his profit must now give way to the advocate of human welfare, who rightly maintains that every man holds his property subject to the general right of the community to regulate its use to whatever degree the public welfare may require it.

But I think we may go still further. The right to regulate the use of wealth in the public interest is universally admitted. Let us admit also the right to regulate the terms and conditions of labor, which is the chief element of wealth, directly in the interest of the common good. The fundamental thing to do for every man is to give him a chance to reach a place in which he will make the greatest possible contribution to the public welfare. Understand what I say there. Give him a chance, not push him up if he will not be pushed. Help any man who stumbles; if he lies down, it is a poor job to try to carry him; but if he is a worthy man, try your best to see that he gets a chance to show the worth that is in him. No man can be a good citizen unless he has a wage more than sufficient to cover the bare cost of living, and hours of labor short enough so after his day's work is done he will have time and energy to bear his share in the management of the community, to help in carrying the general load. We keep countless men from being good citizens by the conditions of life by which we surround them. We need comprehensive workman's compensation acts, both State and national laws to regulate child labor and work for women, and, especially, we need in our common schools not merely education in book-learning, but also practical training for daily life and work. We need to enforce better sanitary conditions for our workers and to extend the use of safety appliances for workers in industry and commerce, both within and between the States. Also, friends, in the interest of the working man himself, we need to set our faces like flint against mob-violence just as against corporate greed; against violence and injustice and lawlessness by wage-workers just as much as against lawless cunning and greed and selfish arrogance of employers. If I could ask but one thing of my fellow countrymen, my request would be that, whenever they go in for reform, they remember the two sides, and that they always exact justice from one side as much as from the other. I have small use for the public servant who can always see and denounce the corruption of the capitalist, but who cannot persuade himself, especially before election, to say a word about lawless mob-violence. And I have equally small use for the man, be he a judge on the bench or editor of a great paper, or wealthy and influential private citizen, who can see clearly enough and denounce the lawlessness of mob-violence, but whose eyes are closed so that he is blind when the question is one of corruption of business on a gigantic scale. Also, remember what I said about excess in reformer and reactionary alike. If the reactionary man, who thinks of nothing but the rights of property, could have his way, he would bring about a revolution; and one of my chief fears in connection with progress comes because I do not want to see our people, for lack of proper leadership, compelled to follow men whose intentions are excellent, but whose eyes are a little too wild to make it really safe to trust them. Here in Kansas there is one paper which habitually denounces me as the tool of Wall Street, and at the same time frantically repudiates the statement that I am a Socialist on the ground that that is an unwarranted slander of the Socialists.

The American people are right in demanding that New Nationalism, without which we cannot hope to deal with new problems. The New Nationalism puts the national need before sectional or personal advantage. It is impatient of the utter confusion that results from local legislatures attempting to treat national issues as local issues. It is still more impatient of the impotence which springs from over division of governmental powers, the impotence which makes it possible for local selfishness or for legal cunning, hired by wealthy special interests, to bring national activities to a deadlock. This New Nationalism regards the executive power as the steward of the public welfare. It demands of the judiciary that it shall be interested primarily in human welfare rather than in property, just as it demands that the representative body shall represent all the people rather than any one class or section of the people.

I believe in shaping the ends of government to protect property as well as human welfare. Normally, and in the long run, the ends are the same; but whenever the alternative must be faced, I am for men and not for property, as you were in the Civil War. I am far from underestimating the importance of dividends; but I rank dividends below human character. Again, I do not have any sympathy with the reformer who says he does not care for dividends. Of course, economic welfare is necessary, for a man must pull his own weight and be able to support his family. I know well that the reformers must not bring upon the people economic ruin, or the reforms themselves will go down in the ruin. But we must be ready to face temporary disaster, whether or not brought on by those who will war against us to the knife. Those who oppose reform will do well to remember that ruin in its worst form is inevitable if our national life brings us nothing better than swollen fortunes for the few and the triumph in both politics and business of a sordid and selfish materialism.

If our political institutions were perfect, they would absolutely prevent the political domination of money in any part of our affairs. We need to make our political representatives more quickly and sensitively responsive to the people whose servants they are. More direct action by the people in their own affairs under proper safeguards is vitally necessary. The direct primary is a step in this direction, if it is associated with a corrupt-services act effective to prevent the advantage of the man willing recklessly and unscrupulously to spend money over his more honest competitor. It is particularly important that all moneys received or expended for campaign purposes should be publicly accounted for, not only after election, but before election as well. Political action must be made simpler, easier, and freer from confusion for every citizen. I believe that the prompt removal of unfaithful or incompetent public servants should be made easy and sure in whatever way experience shall show to be most expedient in any given class of cases.

One of the fundamental necessities in a representative government such as ours is to make certain that the men to whom the people delegate their power shall serve the people by whom they are elected, and not the special interests. I believe that every national officer, elected or appointed, should be forbidden to perform any service or receive any compensation, directly or indirectly, from interstate corporations; and a similar provision could not fail to be useful within the States.

The object of government is the welfare of the people. The material progress and prosperity of a nation are desirable chiefly so long as they lead to the moral and material welfare of all good citizens. Just in proportion as the average man and woman are honest, capable of sound judgment and high ideals, active in public affairs,-but, first of all, sound in their home, and the father and mother of healthy children whom they bring up well,-just so far, and no farther, we may count our civilization a success. We must have-I believe we have already-a genuine and permanent moral awakening, without which no wisdom of legislation or administration really means anything; and, on the other hand, we must try to secure the social and economic legislation without which any improvement due to purely moral agitation is necessarily evanescent. Let me again illustrate by a reference to the Grand Army. You could not have won simply as a disorderly and disorganized mob. You needed generals; you needed careful administration of the most advanced type; and a good commissary-the cracker line. You well remember that success was necessary in many different lines in order to bring about general success. You had to have the administration at Washington good, just as you had to have the administration in the field; and you had to have the work of the generals good. You could not have triumphed without the administration and leadership; but it would all have been worthless if the average soldier had not had the right stuff in him. He had to have the right stuff in him, or you could not get it out of him. In the last analysis, therefore, vitally necessary though it was to have the right kind of organization and the right kind of generalship, it was even more vitally necessary that the average soldier should have the fighting edge, the right character. So it is in our civil life. No matter how honest and decent we are in our private lives, if we do not have the right kind of law and the right kind of administration of the law, we cannot go forward as a nation. That is imperative; but it must be an addition to, and not a substitute for, the qualities that make us good citizens. In the last analysis, the most important elements in any man's career must be the sum of those qualities which, in the aggregate, we speak of as character. If he has not got it, then no law that the wit of man can devise, no administration of the law by the boldest and strongest executive, will avail to help him. We must have the right kind of character-character that makes a man, first of all, a good man in the home, a good father, and a good husband-that makes a man a good neighbor. You must have that, and, then, in addition, you must have the kind of law and the kind of administration of the law which will give to those qualities in the private citizen the best possible chance for development. The prime problem of our nation is to get the right type of good citizenship, and, to get it, we must have progress, and our public men must be genuinely progressive.

DOCUMENT 23

Progressive Party Platform 1912

Resolutions Committee

November 5, 1912

D uring his campaign for the presidency in 1904, Theodore Roosevelt publicly resolved not to run in 1908; instead, he supported his secretary of war,
William Howard Taft, as the Republican nominee. Taft was elected president in
1908, but his conservative politics led to a falling out with Roosevelt, who decided
to return to the political arena in order to oppose his former ally. In the 1912 election, therefore, it was Roosevelt who accepted the nomination of the newly formed
Progressive Party.[1]

The Progressives held a convention in Chicago that was populated by dedicated reformers who wanted to radically remake America. Their numbers included
suffragettes, social workers, urban planners, conservationists, political reformers,
and idealists of all strains. Neither the candidate nor the platform let them down.
Roosevelt's "Confession of Faith" speech and the platform contained plans for a
democratic welfare state, though that state would not fully materialize for another
quarter century. The platform and Roosevelt also called for the reform of political
parties to make them more accountable to the people and less beholden to special
interests. Proposals such as primaries, the initiative, and the referendum were
put forward as alternatives to party procedures. Roosevelt's influence over the
convention was absolute and he brought the crowd to thunderous applause when
he declared, "We stand at Armageddon and we battle for the Lord," followed by
a reverential singing of "The Battle Hymn of the Republic."

SOURCE: Progressive Party Platform 1912, November 5, 1912. Online by Gerhard Peters
and John T. Woolley, *The American Presidency Project*. https://www.presidency.ucsb.edu/
node/273288.

---

[1] Also known as the Bull Moose Party, nicknamed after Theodore Roosevelt who
often said he felt as strong as a bull moose.

The conscience of the people, in a time of grave national problems, has called into being a new party, born of the nation's awakened sense of justice. We of the Progressive party here dedicate ourselves to the fulfillment of the duty laid upon us by our fathers to maintain that government of the people, by the people and for the people whose foundations they laid.

We hold with Thomas Jefferson and Abraham Lincoln that the people are the masters of their constitution, to fulfill its purposes and to safeguard it from those who, by perversion of its intent, would convert it into an instrument of injustice. In accordance with the needs of each generation the people must use their sovereign powers to establish and maintain equal opportunity and industrial justice, to secure which this government was founded and without which no republic can endure. This country belongs to the people who inhabit it. Its resources, its business, its institutions and its laws should be utilized, maintained or altered in whatever manner will best promote the general interest.

It is time to set the public welfare in the first place.

THE OLD PARTIES

Political parties exist to secure responsible government and to execute the will of the people.

From these great tasks both of the old parties have turned aside. Instead of instruments to promote the general welfare, they have become the tools of corrupt interests which use them impartially to serve their selfish purposes. Behind the ostensible government sits enthroned an invisible government, owing no allegiance and acknowledging no responsibility to the people.

To destroy this invisible government, to dissolve the unholy alliance between corrupt business and corrupt politics is the first task of the statesmanship of the day.

The deliberate betrayal of its trust by the Republican party, and the fatal incapacity of the Democratic party to deal with the new issues of the new time, have compelled the people to forge a new instrument of government through which to give effect to their will in laws and institutions.

Unhampered by tradition, uncorrupted by power, undismayed by the magnitude of the task, the new party offers itself as the instrument of the people to sweep away old abuses, to build a new and nobler commonwealth.

A COVENANT WITH THE PEOPLE

This declaration is our covenant with the people, and we hereby bind the party and its candidates in state and nation to the pledges made herein.

THE RULE OF THE PEOPLE

The Progressive party, committed to the principle of government by a self-controlled democracy expressing its will through representatives of the people, pledges itself to secure such alterations in the fundamental law of the several states and of the United States as shall insure the representative character of the government.

In particular, the party declares for direct primaries for the nomination of state and national officers, for nation-wide preferential primaries for candidates for the presidency, for the direct election of United States senators by the people; and we urge on the states the policy of the short ballot, with responsibility to the people secured by the initiative, referendum and recall.

AMENDMENT OF CONSTITUTION

The Progressive party, believing that a free people should have the power from time to time to amend their fundamental law so as to adapt it progressively to the changing needs of the people, pledges itself to provide a more easy and expeditious method of amending the federal constitution.

NATION AND STATE

Up to the limit of the constitution, and later by amendment of the constitution, if found necessary, we advocate bringing under effective national jurisdiction those problems which have expanded beyond reach of the individual states.

It is as grotesque as it is intolerable that the several states should by unequal laws in matter of common concern become competing commercial agencies, barter the lives of their children, the health of their women and the safety and well-being of their working people for the profit of their financial interests.

The extreme insistence on states rights by the Democratic party in the Baltimore platform demonstrates anew its inability to understand the world into which it has survived or to administer the affairs of a union of states which have in all essential respects become one people.

SOCIAL AND INDUSTRIAL JUSTICE

The supreme duty of the nation is the conservation of human resources through an enlightened measure of social and industrial justice. We pledge ourselves to work unceasingly in state and nation for:—

Effective legislation looking to the prevention of industrial accidents, occupational diseases, overwork, involuntary unemployment, and other injurious effects incident to modern industry;

The fixing of minimum safety and health standards for the various occupations, and the exercise of the public authority of state and nation including the federal control over interstate commerce and the taxing power, to maintain such standards;

The prohibition of child labor;

Minimum wage standards for working women, to provide a living scale in all industrial occupations;

The prohibition of night work for women and the establishment of an eight-hour day for women and young persons;

One day's rest in seven for all wake-workers; the eight-hour day in continuous twenty-four-hour industries;

The abolition of the convict contract labor system; substituting a system of prison production for governmental consumption only; and the application of prisoners' earnings to the support of their dependent families;

Publicity as to wages, hours and conditions of labor; full reports upon industrial accidents and diseases, and the opening to public inspection of all tallies, weights, measures and check systems on labor products;

Standards of compensation for death by industrial accident and injury and trade diseases which will transfer the burden of lost earnings from the families of working people to the industry, and thus to the community;

The protection of home life against the hazards of sickness, irregular employment and old age through the adoption of a system of social insurance adapted to American use;

The development of the creative labor power of America by lifting the last load of illiteracy from American youth and establishing continuation schools for industrial education under public control and encouraging agricultural education and demonstration in rural schools;

The establishment of industrial research laboratories to put the methods and discoveries of science at the service of American producers.

We favor the organization of the workers, men and women, as a means of protecting their interests and of promoting their progress . . .

EQUAL SUFFRAGE

The Progressive party, believing that no people can justly claim to be a true democracy which denies political rights on account of sex, pledges itself to the task of securing equal suffrage to men and women alike.

CORRUPT PRACTICES

We pledge our party to legislation that will compel strict limitation on all campaign contributions and expenditures, and detailed publicity of both before as well as after primaries and elections.

PUBLICITY AND PUBLIC SERVICE

We pledge our party to legislation compelling the registration of lobbyists; publicity of committee hearings except on foreign affairs, and recording of all votes in committee; and forbidding federal appointees from holding office in state or national political organizations, or taking part as officers or delegates in political conventions for the nomination of elective state or national officials.

THE COURTS

The Progressive party demands such restriction of the power of the courts as shall leave to the people the ultimate authority to determine fundamental questions of social welfare and public policy. To secure this end, it pledges itself to provide:

1. That when an act, passed under the police power of the state, is held unconstitutional under the state constitution, by the courts, the people, after an ample interval for deliberation, shall have an opportunity to vote on the question whether they desire the act to become a law, notwithstanding such decision.

2. That every decisions of the highest appellate court of a state declaring an act of the legislature unconstitutional on the ground of its violation of

the federal constitution shall be subject to the same review by the Supreme Court of the United States as is now accorded to decisions sustaining such legislation...

CIVIL SERVICE

We condemn the violations of the civil service law under the present administration, including the coercion and assessment of subordinate employees, and the President's refusal to punish such violation after a finding of guilty by his own commission; his distribution of patronage among subservient congressmen, while withholding it from those who refuse support of administration measures; his withdrawal of nominations from the Senate until political support for himself was secured, and his open use of the offices to reward those who voted for his renomination.

To eradicate these abuses, we demand not only the enforcement of the civil service act in letter and spirit, but also legislation which will bring under the competitive system postmasters, collectors, marshals and all other nonpolitical officers, as well as the enactment of an equitable retirement law, and we also insist upon continuous service during good behavior and efficiency...

CONCLUSION

On these principles and on the recognized desirability of uniting the Progressive forces of the nation into an organization which shall unequivocally represent the Progressive spirit and policy we appeal for the support of all American citizens, without regard to previous political affiliations.

Popular Government

William Howard Taft

1913

T aft and Roosevelt drifted apart while Roosevelt was out of the country; when Roosevelt returned, the two men could not make amends. Roosevelt first began expressing disappointment in Taft, and disappointment soon became out-right criticism. Yet Roosevelt gave no hint he would challenge Taft for the Republican nomination until Wisconsin senator La Follette announced a presidential run as a Republican. Roosevelt then moved to position himself for a run as well. When Taft won the nomination at the Republican National Convention, Roosevelt bolted the party and joined the Progressive Party. With the Republican Party now split, Taft realized he had little hope of winning the election. Taft spent as much time on the golf course as he did campaigning, and the race quickly came down to Wilson versus Roosevelt. After losing reelection, Taft accepted an offer to become Kent Professor of Law and Legal History at Yale Law School. There he wrote extensively and gave several notable lectures. He continued his tenure at Yale until President Harding made him Chief Justice of the United States, a position he held until just before his death in 1930.

Taft had a visceral distaste for campaigning and politics. Although the party bosses handed him the nomination in 1912, he detested the world of parties and party politics. Nevertheless, Taft spoke out about Progressive Party reforms and considered them to be worse than the disease. In particular, he took issue with the direct primary and believed it to be a counterfeit way of securing a successful party nomination. Primaries attracted voters who were not really wedded to particular candidates and gave advantage to men of wealth and power over those actually qualified for office. In some states, members of the opposition party could vote in a party's primary, thus undermining the results by opposition party members voting for poorly qualified candidates. None of this, according to Taft, represented a substantial improvement over the existing convention system.

SOURCE: William H. Taft, *Popular Government: Its Essence, Its Permanence, and Its Perils* (New Haven: Yale University Press, 1913), 96—115.

There is one other proposed reform that has been associated with the new methods of initiative, referendum and recall,[1] though not necessarily involving them or involved in them. I mean the direct primary. That is a method of selecting the party candidates to be voted for in the election by a preliminary election of the members of the party. It is also usual and necessary to have a declaration of party principles so that the whole electorate may know what may be expected if the party succeeds in electing its candidates and controls the legislature and the executive. The direct primary itself cannot furnish this, and it is usually accompanied by some plan for securing such a declaration either from a party committee or from a conference of candidates. The same evils which have prompted a resort to such radical methods as the initiative, the referendum and the recall, have also stimulated a wish to change the old methods of party government, of the selection of party candidates, and the declaration of party principles.

... But to return to the party primary. A party is a voluntary organization, and originally the natural theory was that the members of the party should be left to themselves to determine how their party representatives were to be selected and their party principles were to be formulated; but the abuses to which completely voluntary organizations of this kind led, brought about a change of view as to the function of the government with reference to such party procedure.

... The reports leave no doubt whatever, indeed the statistics of the elections frequently conclusively confirm the conclusion, that in State and other primaries, thousands and tens of thousands of Democrats vote at Republican primaries, and vice versa.[2] It often happens that in one party, a primary issue, like the selection of a candidate, is settled in advance by general agreement as to who the candidate shall be or what the principle shall be. In such a case the voters of that party feel entirely free to go into the primaries of the other party, and sometimes, with malice aforethought, to vote for the candidate in that party whom it will be most easy for the candidate of their own party to defeat at the general election.

Of course, this is all wrong. This is not taking the voice of the party. It is

---

[1] The initiative is the right of voters to initiate legislative action. The referendum allows voters to vote on a single political question which has been referred to them for decision. The recall allows voters to vote an elected official out of office before their term of office is up.

[2] As Taft states later on, state courts had ruled in several places that no citizen could be deprived of the right to vote in either primary regardless of party affiliation.

taking the voice of men who are not interested that the party should succeed, and who do not intend to be genuine supporters of the men whom they put upon the party ticket.

... It seems to have been the opinion in the Courts of some States that in carrying on an election of this sort, no citizen, whatever his party, could be deprived of the right to vote in either primary.[3] Such a construction may turn upon peculiar language in a state constitution, but the result is so absurd in the provision for a party primary that it cannot for a moment be sustained on general principles and is utterly at war with fairness and honesty in party control.

Until some method has been devised successfully to prevent this fraud I have been describing, we cannot be said to have a successfully primary law. Of course, it is helpful to have party primaries of all parties on the same day. In this way, if there is a real controversy in all parties, the voters are likely to divide themselves according to their real and sincere party affiliations, because one can only vote in one primary; but the case of a lively fight in one party and none in another is so frequent that the difficulty I have suggested is often a real one.

The first impulse, and a proper one, of the honest legislator, in dealing with this subject, is to give all the members of the party an equal voice in the selection of candidates and in the declaration of party principles. Therefore all the rules which limit the caucus to the active few, or which exclude regular members of the party, have been properly abolished under such primary statutes, and provision is made for every such member to cast his ballot.

The question upon which opinions differ vitally is whether these electors of the party shall cast their ballots directly for their candidates to be run at the general election, or whether they shall select delegates to local conventions, the candidates to be selected in the local conventions. The modern tendency is toward the direct selection of candidates by the party electors themselves, without the intervention of a convention. I am inclined to think that for a time at least this elimination of the party convention in local politics is a good thing.

Theoretically the convention would be better for reasons which can be very shortly stated. If all the electors, divided into wards and precincts, could select honest and intelligent delegates to represent them in a convention, and these delegates were to give their best thought and disinterested effort

---

[3] See Freeman v. Board of Registry & Election of Metuchen, 76 N.J.L. 83 (1907). For a contrary view see Rouse v. Thompson, 228 Ill. 522 (1907).

to the selection of candidates, I have no doubt that the candidates selected would be better for the party and better for the people than the candidates selected directly at a primary. And this is because the delegates can better inform themselves as to the qualifications of the party candidates than can the people at large. And, secondly, the delegates of a party have a sense of responsibility in selecting the party candidates to secure the support of the people at the general election which is utterly absent in the votes which are cast by the electors of the party at the direct primary polls. There the party electors vote for the men who have been brought favorably to their attention by the newspapers and other means of publicity which the candidates themselves are able to adopt and use. They cast their votes very much as the electors at a general election cast their votes, for the men whom they like, or the men whom they know, and frequently without much knowledge or preference at all. Whereas, in a convention, the leaders and the delegates have the keenest care with respect to what is going to happen at the general election.

In the selection of State and national candidates, this becomes a very important matter. One tendency in a direct election of candidates in a national party will be to select a popular partisan, while that of a convention system will be to take a more moderate man whose name will appeal to the independent voter. Thus a primary election in 1860 would certainly have nominated Seward, not Lincoln; in 1876 would have nominated Blaine, not Hayes.[4]

A third objection to the direct election of candidates by the people is the obvious advantage which the men with wealth and of activity and of little modesty, but of great ambition to be candidates, without real qualification for office, have over the men who, having qualifications for office, are either without means or refuse to spend money for such a purpose, and are indisposed to press their own fitness upon the voters. In other words, the direct election of candidates very much reduces the probability that the office will seek the man.

. . . The direct primary puts a premium on self-seeking of an office. After

---

[4] William Seward (1801–1872) was secretary of state from 1861 to 1869 and earlier served as governor of New York and US senator. Abraham Lincoln (1809–1865) was the 16th president of the US and guided the nation through the Civil War until his assassination in 1865. James Blaine (1830–1893) was a Republican politician who served in the US House of Representatives (serving as Speaker from 1869 to 1875) and then later in the Senate. He was nominated for the presidency in 1884 but lost to Democrat Grover Cleveland. Rutherford B. Hayes (1822–1893) was the 19th president of the US from 1877 to 1881.

men are nominated as party candidates, the party is behind them, and can elect them even though they modestly refrain from exploiting themselves. But in the stage previous to this, when the candidates are to be selected at a direct primary for a party, modest but qualified men are never selected. This substantially lessens the number of available candidates capable by reason of their intelligence and experience of filling the offices well.

I have thus stated three serious objections to the direct election of candidates by the people for local offices and for representatives in Congress and the legislature, and yet I do not think that they are sufficient to overcome the present necessity of avoiding the evils that have arisen from the delegate and convention systems so far as these local and district officers are concerned. The delegates selected for the local convention are many of them usually not of a character to resist the blandishments and the corrupt means which will in such cases be used by bosses and the principals of bosses. The local convention of local delegates offers such a rich opportunity for manipulation of those who are corruptible,—things are done so quickly by committees of credentials, and on resolutions,—that the opportunity of the unscrupulous boss in such a convention is very great. I sympathize, therefore, with the movement to abolish the local convention, at least until the exercise of the direct primary shall have broken up the local machines and shall have given an opportunity to the electors of the party, even with the disadvantage of inadequate information, to express their will.

Platform of the National Woman's Party

Party Convention

June 1916

F rom the colonial period forward, women, with or without the vote, had been involved in politics. Women supported or opposed the Revolution through their toil, words, and sacrifices. Women who owned property could vote in a few states for a while. But even without the franchise, women attended rallies, created organizations that aimed at helping underprivileged women and children, and joined reform movements that ranged from abolishing alcohol to ending the scourge of slavery. In 1872, Victoria Woodhull became the first female candidate for president, although she was arrested for trying to cast a vote for herself. The Prohibition Party actually included women at their conventions.

The National Woman's Party (NWP) had its origins in 1912 when Lucy Burns and Alice Paul were appointed to the National American Woman Suffrage Association's (NAWSA) congressional committee. These two women had firsthand experience with the successful use of aggressive tactics such as picketing and public marches by the British suffrage movement and wanted to adopt many of those radical approaches in the United States. In 1914, Alice Paul led a breakaway movement from the NAWSA to form the Congressional Union to pressure the Democratic Party to secure women's right to vote. In 1916, the CU was renamed the National Woman's Party. In June of that year, Paul and a group of like-minded women organized at Chicago's Blackstone Theatre with the goal of creating the first women's political party. Their intention was to distinguish themselves from the existing political parties, and they adopted a platform of one plank: the immediate passage of a federal woman's suffrage amendment. In 1920, their objective was achieved, with the adoption of the Nineteenth Amendment.

SOURCE: "Platform of the National Woman's Party," June 1916. https://archives.iupui.edu/ bitstream/handle/2450/927/mss60-10.pdf?sequence=1.

ADOPTED by a CONVENTION
of WOMEN VOTERS assembled
in the Blackstone Theatre, Chicago
on June 5, 6, and 7, 1916
Miss Anne Martin, Nevada, Chairman
Miss Ella Abeel, Illinois, Secretary

THE National Woman's Party stands for the passage of the amendment to the United States Constitution known as the Susan B. Anthony amendment, proposing an amendment to the Constitution of the United States extending the right of suffrage to women:

Resolved by the Senate and House of Representatives of the United States of America in Congress assembled (two-thirds of each House concurring therein), That the following article be proposed to the legislatures of the several states as an amendment to the Constitution of the United States, which, when ratified by three-fourths of the said legislatures, shall be valid as part of said Constitution, namely:

Article—Sec. 1. The right of citizens of the United States to vote shall not be denied or abridged by the United States or by any state on account of sex.

Sec. 2. Congress shall have power, by appropriate legislation, to enforce the provisions of this article.

The National Woman's Party, convinced that the enfranchisement of women is the paramount issue, pledges itself to use its united vote to secure the passage of the Susan B. Anthony amendment, irrespective of the interests of any national political party, and pledges its unceasing opposition to all who oppose this amendment.

NATIONAL WOMAN'S PARTY
National Headquarters, Lafayette Square, Washington, D. C.

Progressive Party Platform of 1924

Resolutions Committee

November 4, 1924

O f particular interest in the Progressive platform of 1924 was proposed reform of the courts. The Progressives favored a constitutional amendment that would protect congressional legislation from judicial review. They also favored direct popular election of federal judges for a term of no more than ten years, with the election being held without party designation. Senator Robert La Follette became the nominee for the party in 1924 after initially predicting that a third party would not be necessary. La Follette had stated that the only reason a third party would need representation in the election would be if the two major parties nominated reactionaries, or those who stood opposed to Progressive reform ideas. To his mind, however, this is exactly what the Democrats and Republicans did. Twelve hundred delegates and nine thousand spectators ratified the La Follette nomination. La Follette sought to siphon votes from both major parties; in his acceptance speech, he argued for cutting military spending, attacking monopolies, and nationalizing the railroads. He also supported nationalization of several major industries and an increase of taxes on the wealthy.

SOURCE: Progressive Party Platform of 1924, November 4, 1924. Online by Gerhard Peters and John T. Woolley, *The American Presidency Project.* https://www.presidency.ucsb.edu/node/273290.

The great issue before the American people today is the control of government and industry by private monopoly.

For a generation the people have struggled patiently, in the face of repeated betrayals by successive administrations, to free themselves from this intolerable power which has been undermining representative government.

Through control of government, monopoly has crushed competition, stifled private initiative and independent enterprise, and without fear of punishment now exacts extortionate profits upon every necessity of life consumed by the public.

The equality of opportunity proclaimed by the Declaration of Independence and asserted and defended by Jefferson and Lincoln as the heritage of every American citizen has been displaced by special privilege for the few, wrested from the government of the many.

FUNDAMENTAL RIGHTS IN DANGER—That tyrannical power which the American people denied to a king, they will no longer endure from the monopoly system. The people know they cannot yield to any group the control of the economic life of the nation and preserve their political liberties. They know monopoly has its representatives in the halls of congress, on the federal bench, and in the executive departments; that these servile agents barter away the nation's natural resources, nullify acts of congress by judicial veto an administrative favor, invade the people's rights by unlawful arrests and unconstitutional searches and seizures, direct our foreign policy in the interests of predatory wealth, and make wars and conscript the sons of the common people to fight them

The usurpation in recent years by the federal courts of the power to nullify laws duly enacted by the legislative branch of the government is a plain violation of the Constitution.[1] Abraham Lincoln, in his first inaugural address, said: "The candid citizen must confess that if the policy of the government, upon vital questions affecting the whole people, is to be irrevocably fixed by decisions of the supreme court, the people will have ceased to be their own rulers, having to that extent practically resigned their government into the hands of that eminent tribunal." The constitution specifically vests all legislative power in the congress, giving that body power and authority to override the veto of the president. The federal courts are given no authority under the constitution to veto acts of congress. Since the federal courts have assumed to exercise such veto power, it is essential that the Constitution shall give to the congress, the right to over-ride such judicial veto, otherwise the court will make itself master over the other co-ordinate branches of the government. The people themselves must approve or disapprove the present exercise of legislative power by the federal courts.

DISTRESS OF AMERICAN FAMILIES—The present condition of American agriculture constitutes an emergency of the gravest character. The department of commerce report shows that during 1923 there was a steady and marked increase in dividends paid by the great industrial corporations. The same is true of the steam and electric railways and practically all other large corporations. On the other hand, the secretary of agriculture reports

---

[1] See Hammer v. Dagenhart, 247 U.S. 251 (1918).

that in the fifteen principal wheat growing states more than 108,000 farmers since 1920 have lost their farms through foreclosure and bankruptcy; that more than 122,000 have surrendered their property without legal proceedings, and that nearly 375,000 have retained possession of their property only through the leniency of their creditors, making a total of more than 600,000 or 26 per cent of all farmers who have virtually been bankrupted since 1920 in these fifteen states alone.

Almost unlimited prosperity for the great corporations and ruin and bankruptcy for agriculture is the direct and logical result of the politics and legislation which deflated the farmer while extending almost unlimited credit to the great corporations; which protected with exorbitant tariffs the industrial magnates, but depressed the prices of the farmers' products by financial juggling while greatly increasing the cost of what he may buy; which guaranteed excessive freight rates to the railroads and put a premium on wasteful management while saddling an unwarranted burden on to the backs of the American farmer; which permitted gambling in the products of the farm by grain speculators to the great detriments of the farmers and to the great profit of the grain gambler.

A COVENANT WITH THE PEOPLE—Awakened by the dangers which menace their freedom and prosperity the American people still retain the right and courage to exercise their sovereign control over their government. In order to destroy the economic and political power of monopoly, which has come between the people and their government, we pledge ourselves to the following principles and policies:

THE HOUSE CLEANING—1. We pledge a complete housecleaning in the department of justice, the department of the interior, and the other executive departments. We demand that the power of the federal government be used to crush private monopoly, not to foster it.

...RAILROADS—3. We favor repeal of the Esch-Cummins railroad law[2] and the fixing of railroad rates upon the basis of actual, prudent investment and cost of service. We pledge speedy enactment of the Howell-Barkley bill for the adjustment of controversies between railroads and their employees, which was held up in the last congress by joint action of reactionary leaders of the Democratic and Republican parties. We declare for public ownership

---

[2] An act passed in 1920 that returned railroads to private operation after World War I and gave the Interstate Commerce Commission responsibility to ensure profitability.

of railroads with definite safeguards against bureaucratic control, as the only final solution of the transportation problem.

... THE COURTS—5. We favor submitting to the people for their considerate judgment, a constitutional amendment providing that congress may by enacting a statute make it effective over a judicial veto.

We favor such amendment to the Constitution as may be necessary to provide for the election of all federal judges, without party designation, for fixed terms not exceeding ten years, by direct vote of the people.

THE FARMERS—6. We favor drastic reduction of the exorbitant duties on manufactures provided in the Fordney-McCumber tariff legislation,[3] the prohibiting of gambling by speculators and profiteers in agricultural products; the reconstruction of the federal reserve and federal farm loan systems, so as to eliminate control by usurers, speculators and international financiers, and to make the credit of the nation available upon fair terms to all and without discrimination to business men, farmers and homebuilders. We advocate the calling of a special session of congress to pass legislation for the relief of American agriculture. We favor such further legislation as may be needful or helpful in promoting and protecting co-operative enterprises. We demand that the interstate commerce commission proceed forthwith to reduce by an approximation to pre-war levels the present freight rates on agricultural products including live stock, and upon the materials required upon American farms for agricultural purposes.

... WAR VETERANS—9. We favor adjusted compensation for the veterans of the late war, not as charity, but as a matter of right, and we demand that the money necessary to meet this obligation of the government be raised by taxes laid upon wealth in proportion to the ability to pay, and declare our opposition to the sales tax or any other device to shift this obligation onto the backs of the poor in higher prices and increased cost of living. We do not regard the payment at the end of a long period of a small insurance as provided by the law recently passed as in any sense a discharge of the nation's obligations to the veterans of the late war.

GREAT LAKES TO SEA—10. We favor a deep waterway from the Great Lakes to the sea. The government should, in conjunction with Canada, take immediate action to give the northwestern states an outlet to the ocean for cargoes, without change in the bulk, thus making the primary markets on the Great Lakes equal to those of New York.

---

[3] Passed in 1922, it raised American tariffs on numerous imported goods to protect factories and farms.

POPULAR SOVEREIGNTY—11. Over and above constitutions and statutes and greater than all, is the supreme sovereignty of the people, and with them should rest the final decision of all great questions of national policy. We favor such amendments to the federal Constitution as may be necessary to provide for the direct nomination and election of the president, to extend the initiative and referendum to the federal government, and to insure a popular referendum for or against war except in cases of actual invasion.[4]

PEACE ON EARTH—12. We denounce the mercenary system of foreign policy under recent administrations in the interests of financial imperialists, oil monopolists and international bankers, which has at times degraded our state department from its high service as a strong and kindly intermediary of defenseless governments to a trading outpost for those interests and concession-seekers engaged in the exploitations of weaker nations, as contrary to the will of the American people, destructive of domestic development and provocative of war.

---

[4] The initiative is the right of voters to initiate legislative action. The referendum allows voters to vote on a single political question which has been referred to them for decision. The recall allows voters to vote an elected official out of office before their term of office is up.

The Seven Stages of the Office Seeker

John Childs, and Edward Williams Clay, 1852

This satirical print uses the popular folk-art trope of the "life and ages of man" to illustrate the progressive and inevitable corruption of the party-patronage system characteristic of New York politics in the antebellum period. Although the early stages seem innocent enough (treating one's supporter to a drink), it is clear that the artist regards all attempts to persuade voters with appeals to anything other than reason as suspect.

Political Chart: Presidential Campaign

1860

SOURCE: H. H. Lloyds & Co., New York. Photograph.
https://www.loc.gov/item/scsm000926/.

This broadside shows how hotly contested the presidential field was in 1860, highlighting all of the candidates and their party platforms.

Interior of Tammany Hall, New York:
the Democratic Convention in Session
Theodore R. Davis, New York, 1868

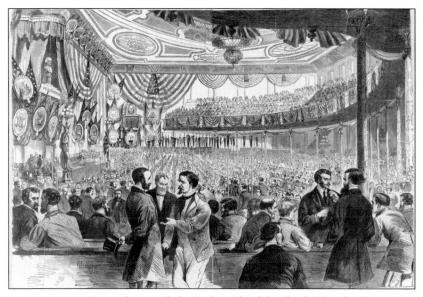

SOURCE: From photographs by Rockwood and sketches by Theodore R.
Davis. New York, 1868. Library of Congress, LC-USZ62-106750.

Arrival of the Delegates to the
Republican Convention in Chicago

1868

SOURCE: Sketch by W. B. Baird, Library of Congress, LC-USZ62-127516.

Elephant and Donkey prior to race to Washington to decide the bet of Joseph Cannon and Frederic Thompson.

Luna Park, Coney Island, NY, c. 1911

National Progressive Convention
Chicago, August 6, 1912

SOURCE: Library of Congress, LC-USZ62-116075/

Balloting for President

c. 1840-1848

SOURCE: New York Public Library Digital Collections, http://digitalcollections. nypl.org/items/510d47e0-cd26-a3d9-e040-e00a18064a99

Editor's note: The original caption to this image reads Inside a polling place: "The voter quietly takes his place in the stream; and, in his turn, finds himself in front of a table or long desk, on which are two small mahogany or green boxes of various shapes, long or square; generally about a foot square, with a little aperture on the top, to receive the folded tickets, and respectively marked S. and E.—S.— State Governor, Members of Assembly, and E. Electors, who are respectively pledged to elect—the Democratic or Whig candidate— President of the United States. Behind the table are two inspectors— one of each party—well-known and reputable citizens, chosen by the mayor. To either of these gentlemen, the voter presents his two folded tickets; giving, at the same time, his name and residence. These the inspector repeats in a loud voice to the crowded room—waits a second or two—and then deposits both tickets into their respective boxes; and the voter retires by an opposite door to that he entered by. This is the usual mode, and all that is necessary; the person and politics of the great mass of voters in each ward being sufficiently well-known to the challengers of both parties, and immediately written down in their betting books by two or three persons stationed near the table—under the head of Whig, Democratic, or Doubtful—so that, by dividing the doubtful in half, a pretty near guess can be arrived at."

G

"The rehabilitation of the Democratic party."

April 15, 1885

THE REHABILITATION OF THE DEMOCRATIC PARTY.
The New Suit (on the Jeffersonian Pattern) doesn't quite fit yet; but we hope he will grow up to it.

SOURCE: Keppler & Schwarzmann, Illus. from *Puck*, v. 17, no. 423, Library of Congress, LC-DIG-ppmsca-28189

Editor's note: The original caption to this image reads The new suit (on the Jeffersonian Pattern) doesn't quite fit yet; but we hope he will grow up to it.

Acceptance Speech

Franklin Delano Roosevelt

July 2, 1932

H erbert Hoover took positive steps to combat the Great Depression, but he
made little political headway for himself or his colleagues in the Republican
party. He seemed cold and remote and was unwilling to take extraordinary steps
to provide direct relief to the American people. This caused Democrats to approach
the coming campaign with anticipation and optimism. From the outset, Governor
Franklin D. Roosevelt was the front-runner in his personal popularity, but he still
had to win the nomination. This is not to say that Roosevelt was the only contender.
Al Smith, the 1928 nominee, was in the race, as was John Nance Garner, Speaker
of the House of Representatives. The first three ballots at the convention produced
no winner; two-thirds of the delegates were needed for nomination. Roosevelt then
struck a deal with Garner, offering him the vice presidency, and, as a result, the
next ballot put Roosevelt over the top. Roosevelt then broke tradition and accepted
the nomination in person.

Roosevelt's party leadership spoke to a more responsible style of parties that
would carry out platforms or proposals presented to the people over the course of
an election. In the process, Roosevelt wanted to overcome the decentralization and
localism of parties, which gave Congress too much control. Instead, he favored
executive-oriented parties that would be organized around national purposes.
Roosevelt, in short, wanted real differences between the parties rather than the
parties resembling two sides of the same coin.

SOURCE: Franklin D. Roosevelt, "Address Accepting the Presidential Nomination at the
Democratic National Convention in Chicago," July 2, 1932. Online by Gerhard Peters
and John T. Woolley, *The American Presidency Project*. https://www.presidency.ucsb.edu/
node/275484.

Chairman Walsh, my friends of the Democratic National Convention of 1932:

...I have many things on which I want to make my position clear at the earliest possible moment in this campaign. That admirable document, the platform which you have adopted, is clear. I accept it 100 percent.

And you can accept my pledge that I will leave no doubt or ambiguity on where I stand on any question of moment in this campaign.

As we enter this new battle, let us keep always present with us some of the ideals of the Party: The fact that the Democratic Party by tradition and by the continuing logic of history, past and present, is the bearer of liberalism and of progress and at the same time of safety to our institutions. And if this appeal fails, remember well, my friends, that a resentment against the failure of Republican leadership—and note well that in this campaign I shall not use the word "Republican Party," but I shall use, day in and day out, the words, "Republican leadership"—the failure of Republican leaders to solve our troubles may degenerate into unreasoning radicalism.

The great social phenomenon of this depression, unlike others before it, is that it has produced but a few of the disorderly manifestations that too often attend upon such times.

Wild radicalism has made few converts, and the greatest tribute that I can pay to my countrymen is that in these days of crushing want there persists an orderly and hopeful spirit on the part of the millions of our people who have suffered so much. To fail to offer them a new chance is not only to betray their hopes but to misunderstand their patience.

To meet by reaction that danger of radicalism is to invite disaster. Reaction is no barrier to the radical. It is a challenge, a provocation. The way to meet that danger is to offer a workable program of reconstruction, and the party to offer it is the party with clean hands.

This, and this only, is a proper protection against blind reaction on the one hand and an improvised, hit-or-miss, irresponsible opportunism on the other.

There are two ways of viewing the Government's duty in matters affecting economic and social life. The first sees to it that a favored few are helped and hopes that some of their prosperity will leak through, sift through, to labor, to the farmer, to the small business man. That theory belongs to the party of Toryism, and I had hoped that most of the Tories left this country in 1776

But it is not and never will be the theory of the Democratic Party. This is no time for fear, for reaction or for timidity. Here and now I invite those nominal Republicans who find that their conscience cannot be squared with the groping and the failure of their party leaders to join hands with us; here and now, in equal measure, I warn those nominal Democrats who squint at the future with their faces turned toward the past, and who feel no responsibility to the demands of the new time, that they are out of step with their Party.

Yes, the people of this country want a genuine choice this year, not a choice between two names for the same reactionary doctrine. Ours must be a party of liberal thought, of planned action, of enlightened international outlook, and of the greatest good to the greatest number of our citizens.

Now it is inevitable—and the choice is that of the times—it is inevitable that the main issue of this campaign should revolve about the clear fact of our economic condition, a depression so deep that it is without precedent in modern history. It will not do merely to state, as do Republican leaders to explain their broken promises of continued inaction, that the depression is worldwide. That was not their explanation of the apparent prosperity of 1928. The people will not forget the claim made by them then that prosperity was only a domestic product manufactured by a Republican President and a Republican Congress. If they claim paternity for the one they cannot deny paternity for the other.

. . . Then came the crash. You know the story. Surpluses invested in unnecessary plants became idle. Men lost their jobs; purchasing power dried up; banks became frightened and started calling loans. Those who had money were afraid to part with it. Credit contracted. Industry stopped. Commerce declined, and unemployment mounted.

And there we are today.

Translate that into human terms. See how the events of the past three years have come home to specific groups of people: first, the group dependent on industry; second, the group dependent on agriculture; third, and made up in large part of members of the first two groups, the people who are called "small investors and depositors." In fact, the strongest possible tie between the first two groups, agriculture and industry, is the fact that the savings and to a degree the security of both are tied together in that third group—the credit structure of the Nation.

. . . Statesmanship and vision, my friends, require relief to all at the same time.

. . . Two years ago the platform on which I ran for Governor the second time contained substantially the same provision. The overwhelming sentiment of the people of my State, as shown by the vote of that year, extends, I know, to the people of many of the other States. I say to you now that from this date on the 18th Amendment is doomed. When that happens, we as Democrats must and will, rightly and morally, enable the States to protect themselves against the importation of intoxicating liquor where such importation may violate their State laws. We must rightly and morally prevent the return of the saloon.

To go back to this dry subject of finance, because it all ties in together—the 18th Amendment has something to do with finance, too—in a comprehensive planning for the reconstruction of the great credit groups, including Government credit, I list an important place for that prize statement of principle in the platform here adopted calling for the letting in of the light of day on issues of securities, foreign and domestic, which are offered for sale to the investing public.

My friends, you and I as common-sense citizens know that it would help to protect the savings of the country from the dishonesty of crooks and from the lack of honor of some men in high financial places. Publicity is the enemy of crookedness.

… In so doing, employment can be given to a million men. That is the kind of public work that is self-sustaining, and therefore capable of being financed by the issuance of bonds which are made secure by the fact that the growth of tremendous crops will provide adequate security for the investment.

Yes, I have a very definite program for providing employment by that means. I have done it, and I am doing it today in the State of New York. I know that the Democratic Party can do it successfully in the Nation. That will put men to work, and that is an example of the action that we are going to have.

… Such a plan as that, my friends, does not cost the Government any money, nor does it keep the Government in business or in speculation.

As to the actual wording of a bill, I believe that the Democratic Party stands ready to be guided by whatever the responsible farm groups themselves agree on. That is a principle that is sound; and again I ask for action.

… That is why we are going to make the voters understand this year that this Nation is not merely a Nation of independence, but it is, if we are to survive, bound to be a Nation of interdependence—town and city, and North and South, East and West. That is our goal, and that goal will be understood by the people of this country no matter where they live.

… Go into the home of the business man. He knows what the tariff has done for him. Go into the home of the factory worker. He knows why goods do not move. Go into the home of the farmer. He knows how the tariff has helped to ruin him.

At last our eyes are open. At last the American people are ready to acknowledge that Republican leadership was wrong and that the Democracy is right.

My program, of which I can only touch on these points, is based upon this simple moral principle: the welfare and the soundness of a Nation depend first upon what the great mass of the people wish and need; and second, whether or not they are getting it.

What do the people of America want more than anything else? To my mind, they want two things: work, with all the moral and spiritual values that go with it; and with work, a reasonable measure of security—security for themselves and for their wives and children. Work and security—these are more than words. They are more than facts. They are the spiritual values, the true goal toward which our efforts of reconstruction should lead. These are the values that this program is intended to gain; these are the values we have failed to achieve by the leadership we now have.

Our Republican leaders tell us economic laws—sacred, inviolable, unchangeable—cause panics which no one could prevent. But while they prate of economic laws, men and women are starving. We must lay hold of the fact that economic laws are not made by nature. They are made by human beings.

Yes, when—not if—when we get the chance, the Federal Government will assume bold leadership in distress relief. For years Washington has alternated between putting its head in the sand and saying there is no large number of destitute people in our midst who need food and clothing, and then saying the States should take care of them, if there are. Instead of planning two and a half years ago to do what they are now trying to do, they kept putting it off from day to day, week to week, and month to month, until the conscience of America demanded action.

I say that while primary responsibility for relief rests with localities now, as ever, yet the Federal Government has always had and still has a continuing responsibility for the broader public welfare. It will soon fulfill that responsibility.

... One word more: Out of every crisis, every tribulation, every disaster, mankind rises with some share of greater knowledge, of higher decency, of purer purpose. Today we shall have come through a period of loose thinking, descending morals, an era of selfishness, among individual men and women and among Nations. Blame not Governments alone for this. Blame ourselves in equal share. Let us be frank in acknowledgment of the truth that many amongst us have made obeisance to Mammon, that the profits of speculation, the easy road without toil, have lured us from the old barricades. To return to higher standards we must abandon the false prophets and seek new leaders of our own choosing.

Never before in modern history have the essential differences between the two major American parties stood out in such striking contrast as they do today. Republican leaders not only have failed in material things, they have failed in national vision, because in disaster they have held out no hope, they have pointed out no path for the people below to climb back to places of security and of safety in our American life.

Throughout the Nation, men and women, forgotten in the political philosophy of the Government of the last years look to us here for guidance and for more equitable opportunity to share in the distribution of national wealth.

On the farms, in the large metropolitan areas, in the smaller cities and in the villages, millions of our citizens cherish the hope that their old standards of living and of thought have not gone forever. Those millions cannot and shall not hope in vain.

I pledge you, I pledge myself, to a new deal for the American people. Let us all here assembled constitute ourselves prophets of a new order of competence and of courage. This is more than a political campaign; it is a call to arms. Give me your help, not to win votes alone, but to win in this crusade to restore America to its own people.

Fireside Chat on Primaries

President Franklin Delano Roosevelt

June 24, 1938

R*oosevelt believed that the success of his administration depended upon his ability to maintain a favorable dialogue with the American people. To that end, Roosevelt sought out innovative ways of shaping American public opinion in order to generate broad public support for his programs. One such innovation was the use of "fireside chats," a series of thirty evening radio addresses between 1933 and 1944. He used these addresses to explain his policies, respond to criticism, silence rumor mongering, and bond with the American people. These chats redefined the relationship between the office and the electorate: his warm manner made people feel closer to the president and reassured by his plans to combat the various crises facing the nation. Although the chats were extremely popular, Roosevelt resisted calls to deliver more such chats for fear that too many would dilute their impact on the American public.*

Ironically, the New Deal movement toward more programmatic party politics made party politics less important. This was an unintended consequence of Roosevelt's use of the direct primary to enforce party discipline. The spread of this campaign innovation put an emphasis on candidates and campaigns rather than on big issues like party principles or platforms. This was particularly true in states with "open" primaries that allowed voters to cast a ballot in any primary regardless of their previous affiliation. In all, Roosevelt's experience with the primaries set the stage for the parties' later struggles with managing primaries and building cohesiveness. And Roosevelt's efforts to lead the nation through the primary process was not successful.

SOURCE: Franklin D. Roosevelt, "Fireside Chat (on Primaries)," June 24, 1938. Online by Gerhard Peters and John T. Wooley, *The American Presidency Project*. https://www.presidency.ucsb.edu/node/208978.

. . . And now following out this line of thought, I want to say a few words about the coming political primaries.

Fifty years ago party nominations were generally made in conventions—a system typified in the public imagination by a little group in a smoke-filled room who made out the party slates.

The direct primary was invented to make the nominating process a more democratic one—to give the party voters themselves a chance to pick their party candidates.

What I am going to say to you tonight does not relate to the primaries of any particular political party, but to matters of principle in all parties—Democratic, Republican, Farmer-Labor, Progressive, Socialist or any other. Let that be clearly understood.

It is my hope that everybody affiliated with any party will vote in the primaries, and that every such voter will consider the fundamental principles for which his party is on record. That makes for a healthy choice between the candidates of the opposing parties on Election Day in November.

An election cannot give a country a firm sense of direction if it has two or more national parties which merely have different names but are as alike in their principles and aims as peas in the same pod.

In the coming primaries in all parties, there will by many clashes between two schools of thought, generally classified as liberal and conservative. Roughly speaking, the liberal school of thought recognizes that the new conditions throughout the world call for new remedies.

Those of us in America who hold to this school of thought, insist that these new remedies can be adopted and successfully maintained in this country under our present form of government if we use government as an instrument of cooperation to provide these remedies. We believe that we can solve our problems through continuing effort, through democratic processes instead of Fascism or Communism. We are opposed to the kind of moratorium on reform which, in effect, is reaction itself.

Be it clearly understood, however, that when I use the word "liberal", I mean the believer in progressive principles of democratic, representative government and not the wild man who, in effect, leans in the direction of Communism, for that is just as dangerous as Fascism.

The opposing or conservative school of thought, as a general proposition, does not recognize the need for Government itself to step in and take action to meet these new problems. It believes that individual initiative and private philanthropy will solve them—that we ought to repeal many of the things we have done and go back, for instance, to the old gold standard, or stop all this business of old age pensions and unemployment insurance, or repeal the

Securities and Exchange Act, or let monopolies thrive unchecked—return, in effect, to the kind of Government we had in the twenties.

Assuming the mental capacity of all the candidates, the important question which it seems to me the primary voter must ask is this: "To which of these general schools of thought does the candidate belong"?

As President of the United States, I am not asking the voters of the country to vote for Democrats next November as opposed to Republicans or members of any other party. Nor am I, as President, taking part in Democratic primaries.

As the head of the Democratic Party, however, charged with the responsibility of carrying out the definitely liberal declaration of principles set forth in the 1936 Democratic platform, I feel that I have every right to speak in those few instances where there may be a clear issue between candidates for a Democratic nomination involving these principles, or involving a clear misuse of my own name.

Do not misunderstand me. I certainly would not indicate a preference in a State primary merely because a candidate, otherwise liberal in outlook, had conscientiously differed with me on any single issue. I should be far more concerned about the general attitude of a candidate toward present day problems and his own inward desire to get practical needs attended to in a practical way. We all know that progress may be blocked by outspoken reactionaries and also by those who say "*yes*" to a progressive objective, *but* who always find some reason to oppose any specific proposal to gain that objective. I call that type of candidate a "yes, but" fellow.

And I am concerned about the attitude of a candidate or his sponsors with respect to the rights of American citizens to assemble peaceably and to express publicly their views and opinions on important social and economic issues. There can be no constitutional democracy in any community which denies to the individual his freedom to speak and worship as he wishes. The American people will not be deceived by anyone who attempts to suppress individual liberty under the pretense of patriotism.

This being a free country with freedom of expression—especially with freedom of the press—there will be a lot of mean blows struck between now and Election Day. By "blows" I mean misrepresentation, personal attack and appeals to prejudice. It would be a lot better, of course, if campaigns everywhere could be waged with arguments instead of blows.

I hope the liberal candidates will confine themselves to argument and not resort to blows. In nine cases out of ten the speaker or writer who, seeking to influence public opinion, descends from calm argument to unfair blows hurts himself more than his opponent.

The Chinese have a story on this—a story based on three or four thousand years of civilization: Two Chinese coolies were arguing heatedly in the midst of a crowd. A stranger expressed surprise that no blows were being struck. His Chinese friend replied; "The man who strikes first admits that his ideas have given out."

I know that neither in the summer primaries nor in the November elections will the American voters fail to spot the candidate whose ideas have given out.

Platform of the States Rights Democratic Party

Resolutions Committee

August 14, 1948

I n the 1948 presidential election, Southern Democrats walked out of the Democratic National Convention to protest the party's decision to embrace a civil
rights platform. These defectors then met in Birmingham, Alabama, and formed
their own political party named the States Rights Democratic Party, although
over time they would more commonly be referred to as the Dixiecrats.

The main goal of the party was continued racial segregation in the South and
a buttressing of the Jim Crow laws that supported racial segregation. Governor
Strom Thurmond was selected as the party's presidential nominee. The Dixiecrats
knew they had hardly any chance of winning the election, but they hoped to siphon
off enough votes from the Democratic Party to force a runoff election in the House
of Representatives. There they could extract concessions from either Democrat
Harry Truman or Republican Thomas E. Dewey in exchange for Dixiecrat support. Most Southern Democratic leaders refused to support the party, however,
and the Dixiecrats were able to do little to influence the outcome of the election.

Although the Dixiecrats failed to perform well in the election, they did serve
to put the Democratic Party on notice that it could no longer rely on a solid South
in elections. The South had supported every Democratic candidate since the Civil
War, but that unbroken support was now in question, and in the future, Southern
Democratic voters began looking elsewhere for candidates and parties to support.
Over time, Southern whites made a slow transition to the Republican Party as
Democrats seemed to be increasingly hostile to their views and interests. Democrats, in turn, had to branch out to find new areas of support to counteract the
loss of their Southern brethren.

SOURCE: Platform of the States Rights Democratic Party, August 14, 1948. Online by Gerhard Peters and John T. Woolley, *The American Presidency Project.* https://www.presidency.
ucsb.edu/node/273454.

Unanimously Adopted at Oklahoma City, August 14, 1948

−1−

We believe that the Constitution of the United States is the greatest charter of human liberty ever conceived by the mind of man.

−2−

We oppose all efforts to invade or destroy the rights guaranteed by it to every citizen of this republic.

−3−

We stand for social and economic justice, which, we believe can be guaranteed to all citizens only by a strict adherence to our Constitution and the avoidance of any invasion or destruction of the constitutional rights of the states and individuals. We oppose the totalitarian, centralized bureaucratic government and the police nation called for by the platforms adopted by the Democratic and Republican Conventions.

−4−

We stand for the segregation of the races and the racial integrity of each race; the constitutional right to choose one's associates; to accept private employment without governmental interference, and to earn one's living in any lawful way. We oppose the elimination of segregation, the repeal of miscegenation statutes, the control of private employment by Federal bureaucrats called for by the misnamed civil rights program. We favor home-rule, local self-government and a minimum interference with individual rights.

−5−

We oppose and condemn the action of the Democratic Convention in sponsoring a civil rights program calling for the elimination of segregation, social equality by Federal fiat, regulations of private employment practices, voting, and local law enforcement.

−6−

We affirm that the effective enforcement of such a program would be utterly destructive of the social, economic and political life of the Southern people, and of other localities in which there may be differences in race, creed or national origin in appreciable numbers.

-7-

We stand for the check and balances provided by the three departments of our government. We oppose the usurpation of legislative functions by the executive and judicial departments. We unreservedly condemn the effort to establish in the United States a police nation that would destroy the last vestige of liberty enjoyed by a citizen.

-8-

We demand that there be returned to the people to whom of right they belong, those powers needed for the preservation of human rights and the discharge of our responsibility as democrats for human welfare. We oppose a denial of those by political parties, a barter or sale of those rights by a political convention, as well as any invasion of violation of those rights by the Federal Government. We call upon all Democrats and upon all other loyal Americans who are opposed to totalitarianism at home and abroad to unite with us in ignominiously defeating Harry S. Truman, Thomas E. Dewey and every other candidate for public office who would establish a Police Nation in the United States of America.

-9-

We, therefore, urge that this Convention endorse the candidacies of J. Strom Thurmond and Fielding H. Wright for the President and Vice-president, respectively, of the United States of America.

"Great Society" Speech

President Lyndon B. Johnson

May 22, 1964

T he Great Society, the largest expansion of the welfare state since the New Deal, was the idea of President Lyndon Johnson. The primary goals of the Great Society were to eliminate racial inequality and bring an end to poverty. Johnson advocated massive new spending programs for things such as equal education for all, medical care for all Americans, urban renewal, combating rural poverty, and improving transportation.

Johnson's first public articulation of the Great Society took place in Ohio on May 7, 1964, at Ohio University. There he presented an outline of the plan and its objectives. He delivered a more detailed speech at the University of Michigan in Ann Arbor on May 22, 1964. In years to come, foreign policy would come to overshadow Johnson's Great Society programs and make them increasingly hard to pay for. But his ideas would persist and would be carried forward into subsequent administrations.

Johnson had been a longtime senator, serving as Senate majority leader from 1955 to 1961. During that time, Johnson became a master of party and parliamentary politics and used his immense personal influence to secure passage of key pieces of legislation. As president, Johnson continued to utilize his knowledge of party politics to get his Great Society programs passed by Congress. But keeping his party in line proved extremely challenging. Johnson wanted to be a national leader and he deserves credit for fighting racial discrimination and poverty. But he also wanted to instill a new sense of politics that surpassed the New Deal, and his difficulties acting as party leader made this nearly impossible. Eventually, opponents of the Vietnam War and participants in the youth movements gained power in the Democratic Party and shook Johnson's control. He chose not to seek reelection in 1968.

SOURCE: "Remarks at the University of Michigan," May 22, 1964. Online by Gerhard Peters and John T. Woolley, *The American Presidency Project*. https://www.presidency.ucsb.edu/node/239689.

... The purpose of protecting the life of our Nation and preserving the liberty of our citizens is to pursue the happiness of our people. Our success in that pursuit is the test of our success as a Nation.

For a century we labored to settle and to subdue a continent. For half a century we called upon unbounded invention and untiring industry to create an order of plenty for all of our people.

The challenge of the next half century is whether we have the wisdom to use that wealth to enrich and elevate our national life, and to advance the quality of our American civilization.

Your imagination, your initiative, and your indignation[1] will determine whether we build a society where progress is the servant of our needs, or a society where old values and new visions are buried under unbridled growth. For in your time we have the opportunity to move not only toward the rich society and the powerful society, but upward to the Great Society.

The Great Society rests on abundance and liberty for all. It demands an end to poverty and racial injustice, to which we are totally committed in our time. But that is just the beginning.

The Great Society is a place where every child can find knowledge to enrich his mind and to enlarge his talents. It is a place where leisure is a welcome chance to build an reflect, not a feared cause of boredom and restlessness. It is a place where the city of man serves not only the needs of the body and the demands of commerce but the desire for beauty and the hunger for community.

It is a place where man can renew contact with nature. It is a place which honors creation for its own sake and for what it adds to the understanding of the race. It is a place where men are more concerned with the quality of their goals than the quantity of their goods.

But most of all, the Great Society is not a safe harbor, a resting place, a final objective, a finished work. It is a challenge constantly renewed, beckoning us toward a destiny where the meaning of our lives matches the marvelous products of our labor.

So I want to talk to you today about three places where we begin to build the Great Society—in our cities, in our countryside, and in our classrooms.

Many of you will live to see the day, perhaps 50 years from now, when there will be 400 million Americans—four-fifths of them in urban areas. In the remainder of this century urban population will double, city land will

---

[1] It is likely Johnson uses the word "indignation" here to refer to the sense of outrage he wants people to have about injustice, poverty, racism, and other societal ills.

double, and we will have to build homes, highways, and facilities equal to all those built since this country was first settled. So in the next 40 years we must rebuild the entire urban United States.

Aristotle said: "Men come together in cities in order to live, but they remain together in order to live the good life." It is harder and harder to live the good life in American cities today.

The catalog of ills is long: there is the decay of the centers and the despoiling of the suburbs. There is not enough housing for our people or transportation for our traffic. Open land is vanishing and old landmarks are violated.

Worst of all expansion is eroding the precious and time-honored values of community with neighbors and communion with nature. The loss of these values breeds loneliness and boredom and indifference.

Our society will never be great until our cities are great. Today the frontier of imagination and innovation is inside those cities and not beyond their borders.

New experiments are already going on. It will be the task of your generation to make the American city a place where future generations will come, not only to live but to live the good life.

I understand that if I stayed here tonight I would see that Michigan students are really doing their best to live the good life.

This is the place where the Peace Corps was started. It is inspiring to see how all of you, while you are in this country, are trying so hard to live at the level of the people.

A second place where we begin to build the Great Society is in our countryside. We have always prided ourselves on being not only America the strong and America the free, but America the beautiful. Today that beauty is in danger. The water we drink, the food we eat, the very air that we breathe, are threatened with pollution. Our parks are overcrowded, our seashores overburdened. Green fields and dense forests are disappearing.

A few years ago, we were greatly concerned about the "Ugly American." Today we must act to prevent an ugly America.

For once the battle is lost, once our natural splendor is destroyed, it can never be recaptured. And once man can no longer walk with beauty or wonder at nature his spirit will wither and his sustenance be wasted.

A third place to build the Great Society is in the classrooms of America. There your children's lives will be shaped. Our society will not be great until every young mind is set free to scan the farthest reaches of thought and imagination. We are still far from that goal.

Today, 8 million adult Americans, more than the entire population of

Michigan, have not finished 5 years of school. Nearly 20 million have not finished 8 years of school. Nearly 54 million—more than one-quarter of all America—have not even finished high school

Each year more than 100,000 high school graduates, with proved ability, do not enter college because they cannot afford it. And if we cannot educate today's youth, what will we do in 1970 when elementary school enrollment will be 5 million greater than 1960? And high school enrollment will rise by 5 million. College enrollment will increase by more than 3 million.

In many places, classrooms are overcrowded and curricula are outdated. Most of our qualified teachers are underpaid, and many of our paid teachers are unqualified. So we must give every child a place to sit and a teacher to learn from. Poverty must not be a bar to learning, and learning must offer an escape from poverty.

But more classrooms and more teachers are not enough. We must seek an educational system which grows in excellence as it grows in size. This mean better training for our teachers. It means preparing youth to enjoy their hours of leisure as well as their hours of labor. It means exploring new techniques of teaching, to find new ways to stimulate the love of learning and the capacity for creation.

These are three of the central issues of the Great Society. While our Government has many programs directed at those issues, I do not pretend that we have the full answer to these problems.

But I do promise this: We are going to assemble the best thought and the broadest knowledge from all over the world to find those answers for America. I intend to establish working groups to prepare a series of White House conferences and meetings—on the cities, on natural beauty, on the quality of education, and on other emerging challenges. And from these meetings and from this inspiration and from these studies we will begin to set our course toward the Great Society.

The solution to these problems does not rest on a massive program in Washington, nor can it rely solely on the strained resources of local authority. They require us to create new concepts of cooperation, a creative federalism, between the National Capital and the leaders of local communities.

Woodrow Wilson[2] once wrote: "Every man sent out from his university should be a man of his Nation as well as a man of his time." Within

---

[2] Woodrow Wilson (1856–1924) was the 28th president of the United States, serving from 1913 to 1921. During that time he led America through World War I.

your lifetime powerful forces, already loosed, will take us toward a way of life beyond the realm of our experience, almost beyond the bounds of our imagination.

For better or for worse, your generation has been appointed by history to deal with those problems and to lead America toward a new age. You have the chance never before afforded to any people in any age. You can help build a society where the demands of morality, and the needs of the spirit, can be realized in the life of the Nation.

So, will you join in the battle to give every citizen the full equality which God enjoins and the law requires, whatever his belief, or race, or the color of his skin?

Will you join in the battle to give every citizen an escape from the crushing weight of poverty?

Will you join in the battle to make it possible for all nations to live in enduring peace—as neighbors and not as mortal enemies?

Will you join in the battle to build the Great Society, to prove that our material progress is only the foundation of which we will build a richer life of mind and spirit?

There are those timid souls who say this battle cannot be won; that we are condemned to a soulless wealth. I do not agree. We have the power to shape the civilization that we want. But we need your will, your labor, your hearts, if we are to build that kind of society.

Those who came to this land sought to build more than just a new country. They sought a new world. So I have come here today to your campus to say that you can make their vision our reality. So let us from this moment begin our work so that in the future men will look back and say: It was then, after a long and weary way, that man turned the exploits of his genius to the full enrichment of his life.

Thank you. Goodbye.

Acceptance Speech

Barry Goldwater

July 16, 1964

G oldwater's candidacy represented the coalescing of several conservative social movements that united behind his nomination in 1964. Such movements included Goldwaterites, traditionalists, and neo-conservatives. Some of these groups were reacting to the New Deal, while others represented a rejection of Johnson's Great Society programs.

Regionally, the conservative movement was strongest in the West: Goldwater, a Westerner himself, shared with other Westerners a fear and resentment of the growing power of the federal government to interfere with economic and social life. He and his followers also disliked the treatment of small businessmen by government bureaucrats and they espoused a libertarian view of economics and social policy. Goldwater was also staunchly pro-military, believing that Communism and the Soviet Union posed a direct threat to the future of the United States. Although Goldwater was thoroughly defeated in the election, he succeeded in rejecting the conservatism of the post–New Deal Era that largely agreed with liberal policies or at best criticized them only at the margins.

Goldwater's candidacy reflected a change in the makeup of the Republican Party. LBJ and the revival of liberalism gave rise to a new kind of conservative social movement, one more devoted to ideology than to party but willing to make a national party its instrument. This movement politics that was passionately devoted to right-wing ideology had attempted to spread its influence for some time. But it was in 1964 that these social movements saw their greatest victory in the nomination of Goldwater, who stood for ideas, not the same failed policies of the previous years. The conservative social movements saw in his nomination the fruition of years of hard work and effort. Moreover, Goldwater's nomination would begin the Republican Party's slow turn to the ideological right wing. In contrast, liberal social movements inspired by the counterculture and opposition to the Vietnam War made a liberal version of movement politics a powerful force in the Democratic Party in 1968.

SOURCE: Address Accepting the Presidential Nomination at the Republican National Convention in San Francisco, July 16, 1964. Online by Gerhard Peters and John T. Woolley, *The American Presidency Project*. https://www.presidency.ucsb.edu/node/216657.

... Rather than useful jobs in our country, people have been offered bureaucratic "make work," rather than moral leadership, they have been given bread and circuses, spectacles, and, yes, they have even been given scandals. Tonight there is violence in our streets, corruption in our highest offices, aimlessness among our youth, anxiety among our elders and there is a virtual despair among the many who look beyond material success for the inner meaning of their lives. Where examples of morality should be set, the opposite is seen. Small men, seeking great wealth or power, have too often and too long turned even the highest levels of public service into mere personal opportunity.

Now, certainly, simple honesty is not too much to demand of men in government. We find it in most. Republicans demand it from everyone. They demand it from everyone no matter how exalted or protected his position might be. The growing menace in our country tonight, to personal safety, to life, to limb and property, in homes, in churches, on the playgrounds, and places of business, particularly in our great cities, is the mounting concern, or should be, of every thoughtful citizen in the United States.

Security from domestic violence, no less than from foreign aggression, is the most elementary and fundamental purpose of any government, and a government that cannot fulfill that purpose is one that cannot long command the loyalty of its citizens. History shows us—demonstrates that nothing - nothing prepares the way for tyranny more than the failure of public officials to keep the streets from bullies and marauders.

Now, we Republicans see all this as more, much more, than the rest: of mere political differences or mere political mistakes. We see this as the result of a fundamentally and absolutely wrong view of man, his nature and his destiny. Those who seek to live your lives for you, to take your liberties in return for relieving you of yours, those who elevate the state and downgrade the citizen must see ultimately a world in which earthly power can be substituted for divine will, and this Nation was founded upon the rejection of that notion and upon the acceptance of God as the author of freedom.

Those who seek absolute power, even though they seek it to do what they regard as good, are simply demanding the right to enforce their own version of heaven on earth. And let me remind you, they are the very ones who always create the most hellish tyrannies. Absolute power does corrupt, and those who seek it must be suspect and must be opposed. Their mistaken course stems from false notions of equality, ladies and gentlemen. Equality, rightly understood, as our founding fathers understood it, leads to liberty and to the emancipation of creative differences. Wrongly understood, as it has been so tragically in our time, it leads first to conformity and then to despotism.

Fellow Republicans, it is the cause of Republicanism to resist concentrations of power, private or public, which enforce such conformity and inflict such despotism. It is the cause of Republicanism to ensure that power remains in the hands of the people. And, so help us God, that is exactly what a Republican president will do with the help of a Republican Congress.

It is further the cause of Republicanism to restore a clear understanding of the tyranny of man over man in the world at large. It is our cause to dispel the foggy thinking which avoids hard decisions in the illusion that a world of conflict will somehow mysteriously resolve itself into a world of harmony, if we just don't rock the boat or irritate the forces of aggression—and this is hogwash.

. . . We Republicans see in our constitutional form of government the great framework which assures the orderly but dynamic fulfillment of the whole man, and we see the whole man as the great reason for instituting orderly government in the first place.

We see, in private property and in economy based upon and fostering private property, the one way to make government a durable ally of the whole man, rather than his determined enemy. We see in the sanctity of private property the only durable foundation for constitutional government in a free society. And beyond that, we see, in cherished diversity of ways, diversity of thoughts, of motives and accomplishments. We do not seek to lead anyone's life for him—we seek only to secure his rights and to guarantee him opportunity to strive, with government performing only those needed and constitutionally sanctioned tasks which cannot otherwise be performed.

We Republicans seek a government that attends to its inherent responsibilities of maintaining a stable monetary and fiscal climate, encouraging a free and a competitive economy and enforcing law and order. Thus do we seek inventiveness, diversity, and creativity within a stable order, for we Republicans define government's role where needed at many, many levels, preferably through the one closest to the people involved.

Our towns and our cities, then our counties, then our states, then our regional contacts - and only then, the national government. That, let me remind you, is the ladder of liberty, built by decentralized power. On it also we must have balance between the branches of government at every level.

Balance, diversity, creativity—these are the elements of Republican equation. Republicans agree, Republicans agree heartily to disagree on many, many of their applications, but we have never disagreed on the basic fundamental issues of why you and I are Republicans.

This is a party, this Republican Party, a Party for free men, not for blind followers, and not for conformists.

... I would remind you that extremism in the defense of liberty is no vice. And let me remind you also that moderation in the pursuit of justice is no virtue.

The beauty of the very system we Republicans are pledged to restore and revitalize, the beauty of this Federal system of ours is in its reconciliation of diversity with unity. We must not see malice in honest differences of opinion, and no matter how great, so long as they are not inconsistent with the pledges we have given to each other in and through our Constitution. Our Republican cause is not to level out the world or make its people conform in computer regimented sameness. Our Republican cause is to free our people and light the way for liberty throughout the world.

Ours is a very human cause for very humane goals.

This Party, its good people, and its unquestionable devotion to freedom, will not fulfill the purposes of this campaign which we launch here now until our cause has won the day, inspired the world, and shown the way to a tomorrow worthy of all our yesteryears.

I repeat, I accept your nomination with humbleness, with pride, and you and I are going to fight for the goodness of our land. Thank you.

"Speech at Madison Square Garden"

George Wallace

October 24, 1968

G eorge Wallace ran as a third-party candidate in 1968 for the American
Independent Party. Wallace had been elected governor of Alabama in 1962,
*promising in his inaugural address to maintain "segregation now, segregation
tomorrow, segregation forever." When a federal court ordered the University of
Alabama to admit black students, Wallace stood at the door to the school, vowing
to bar the students' admission. This lasted until President Kennedy federalized
the National Guard and a deputy attorney general ordered Wallace to stand
aside. These actions gave Wallace a national reputation as a fierce opponent of
forced integration, and in 1968 he decided to test his appeal outside of the South.*

*Running with Curtis LeMay as his running mate, Wallace campaigned
throughout the country—the last third-party candidate to actually win states in
the presidential election. His campaign denounced the courts, civil rights legislation, big government, and leniency toward criminals. In the end, however, Wallace's showing was not particularly impressive; he won only five states in the deep
South while taking 13.5% of the popular vote. However, Wallace's candidacy did
demonstrate considerable national opposition to the two major political parties.
Wallace attempted to exploit this discontent by regularly announcing that there
was not a "dime's worth of difference" between the Republicans and the Democrats, and he played upon national discontent with integration, rising taxes, and
bureaucracy. Although he lost the election by a wide margin, Wallace showed that
the parties were somewhat out of touch with the American electorate and were
thus vulnerable to a strong third-party showing by the right candidate. Wallace
was not that candidate, but the major parties had learned a lesson about listening
to their grassroots.*

SOURCE: George Wallace, "Speech at Madison Square Garden, October 24, 1968," in *History
of U.S. Political Parties*, ed. Arthur Schlesinger, vol. 4, *1945–1972: The Politics of Change* (New
York: Chelsea House, 1973), 3491–3497.

... Our system is under attack: the property system, the free enterprise system, and local government. Anarchy prevails today in the streets of the large cities of our country, making it unsafe for you to even go to a political rally here in Madison Square Garden, and that is a sad commentary. Both national parties in the last number of years have kowtowed to every anarchist that has roamed the streets. I want to say before I start on this any longer, that I'm not talking about race. The overwhelming majority of all races in this country are against this breakdown of law and order as much as those who are assembled here tonight. It's a few anarchists, a few activists, a few militants, a few revolutionaries, and a few Communists. But your day, of course is going to be over soon. The American people are not going to stand by and see the security of our nation imperiled, and they're not going to stand by and see this nation destroyed, I can assure you that.

The liberals and the left-wingers in both national parties have brought us to the domestic mess we are in now. And also this foreign mess we are in.

You need to read the book "How to Behave in a Crowd." You really don't know how to behave in a crowd, do you?

Yes, the liberals and left-wingers in both parties have brought us to the domestic mess we are in also to the foreign policy mess we find our nation involved in at the present time, personified by the no-win war in Southeast Asia.

Now what are some of the things we are going to do when we become president? We are going to turn back to you, the people of the states, the right to control our domestic institutions. Today you cannot even go to the school systems of the large cities of our country without fear. This is a sad day when in the greatest city in the world, there is fear not only in Madison Square Garden, but in every school building in the state of New York, and especially in the City of New York. Why has the leadership of both national parties kowtowed to this group of anarchists that makes it unsafe for your child and for your family? I don't understand it. But I can assure you of this—that there's not ten cents worth of difference with what the national parties say other than our party. Recently they say most of the same things we say. I remember six years ago when this anarchy movement started, Mr. Nixon said: "It's a great movement," and Mr. Humphrey said: "It's a great movement." Now when they try to speak and are heckled down, they stand up and say: "We've got to have some law and order in this country." They ought to give you law and order back for nothing, because they have helped to take it away from you, along with the Supreme Court of our country that's made up of Republicans and Democrats.

It's costing the taxpayers of New York and the other states in the union almost a half billion dollars to supervise the schools, hospitals, seniority and apprenticeship lists of labor unions, and businesses. Every year on the federal level we have passed a law that would jail you without a trial by jury about the sale of your own property. Mr. Nixon and Mr. Humphrey, both three or four weeks ago, called for the passage of a bill on the federal level that would require you to sell or lease your own property to whomsoever they thought you ought to lease it to. I say that when Mr. Nixon and Mr. Humphrey succumb to the blackmail of a few anarchists in the streets who said we're going to destroy this country if you do not destroy that adage that a man's home is his castle, they are not fit to lead the American people during the next four years in our country. When I become your president, I am going to ask that Congress repeal this so-called open occupancy law and we're going to, within the law, turn back to the people of every state their public school system. Not one dime of your federal money is going to be used to bus anybody any place that you don't want them to be bussed in New York or any other state.

Yes, the theoreticians and the pseudo-intellectuals have just about destroyed not only local government but the school systems of our country. That's all right. Let the police handle it. So let us talk about law and order. We don't have to talk about it much up here. You understand what I'm talking about in, of course, the City of New York, but let's talk about it.

... You had better be thankful for the police and the firemen of this country. If it were not for them, you couldn't even ride in the streets, much less walk in the streets, of our large cities. Yes, the Kerner Commission Report,[1] recently written by Republicans and Democrats, said that you are to blame for the breakdown of law and order, and that the police are to blame. Well, you know, of course, you aren't to blame. They said we have a sick society. Well, we don't have any sick society. We have a sick Supreme Court and some sick politicians in Washington, - that's who's sick in our country. The Supreme Court of our country has ruled that you cannot even say a simple prayer in a public school, but you can send obscene literature though the mail, and recently they ruled that a Communist can work in a defense plant. But when

---

[1] The Kerner Commission produced the "Report of the National Advisory Commission on Civil Disorders" that looked into the causes of recent rioting in major cities. The Commission blamed the violence on white racism and lack of economic opportunities for black people. The report also called for diversifying police forces and making them more sensitive to the plight of black Americans, along with major investment efforts into housing and creating jobs.

I become your president, we're going to take every Communist out of every defense plant in the United States, I can assure you.

...We are in Vietnam whether you like it or not. I sincerely hope and pray that the conflict is soon over, but we should have learned one thing about our involvement in Southeast Asia—the same thing that Mr. Humphrey now says in his speeches: we should not march alone. I said last year in California that we should never have gone to Vietnam—by ourselves. We should have looked our allies in the face in Western Europe and our non-Communist Asian Allies and said to them: it is as much your interest as it is ours and you are going to go with manpower, munitions, and money, and if you don't go and help us in Southeast Asia, and if you don't stop trading with the North Vietnamese who are killing American servicemen, we are not only going to cut off every dime of foreign aid you're getting, but we're going to ask you to pay back all you owe us from World War I right on this very day.

...I sincerely hope and pray that we have a successful negotiated peace. Well, I'll drown them out, come on. I sincerely hope and pray that we have an honorably negotiated peace to arise out of the Paris peace talks. I know that you pray that, and that the American servicemen can come home. But if we fail diplomatically and politically in Southeast Asia, we're not going to stay there forever, we're not going to see hundreds of American servicemen killed every week for years and months to come. If we do not win diplomatically and politically in Paris, that is, by honorable conclusion of the war, then in my judgment, we ought to end it militarily with conventional weapons and bring the American servicemen home. If we cannot settle it diplomatically and politically, and could not win it militarily with conventional weapons, then I wonder why we're there in the first place? We're going to conclude this way one way or the other either through honorable negotiations or conventional military power.

...My friends, let me say this. We can win this election because it only takes a plurality to win when there are three or more running. If we get thirty-four percent of the vote in this state, and the other two get thirty-three percent apiece, then we win the entire electoral vote of the State of New York. That's all it takes. You know this, and that's one reason Mr. Nixon doesn't want to debate. Well, I want to tell Mr. Nixon it's a good thing he doesn't debate because if he ever does, we're going to point out that he's made so many inconsistent statements about so many matters, I would be happy to debate. But he cannot get a debate started.

...Well, don't worry what the newspapers say about us. Everything I've said tonight is logical and reasonable and constitutional. Not a single thing have I said tonight that anybody can argue logically with, and that's the reason they call us extremists and want to say we're Fascists. They cannot argue with the logic of the position we take here in Madison Square Garden tonight. They want to say, well, they're evil folks. I want to tell these newspapers something. These large newspapers that think they know more than the average citizen on the street of New York haven't always been right. I remember the time the *New York Times* said that Mao tse-Tung was a good man, and he turned out to be a Communist. I remember when they said that Ben Bella[2] was a good man, and he turned out to be a Communist. When old Castro was in the hills of Cuba, the *New York Times* said he was the Robin Hood of the Caribbean, and they introduced him on national television as the George Washington of Cuba. They were mistaken about Castro.

---

[2] Algerian revolutionary who became president of Algeria in 1963 and brought about a number of socialist-style reforms.

"Mandate for Reform" on Party Structure and Delegate Selection

McGovern-Fraser Commission

September 22, 1971

T*he 1968 presidential election was a disaster for the Democrats, largely as a result of their nomination process. In an unusual turn of events, Senator Hubert H. Humphrey won the nomination without having entered any of the primaries. At the convention, Humphrey garnered all his support from unpledged delegates (delegates who were not directed to vote for a particular candidate through the primary process). The result of this disregard for the party's popular choice was a convention that ended in disarray and a badly divided Democratic Party. Student groups protested the convention, resulting in violent clashes in the streets with police.*

To prevent the events of 1968 from happening again, the Democrats established the Commission on Party Structure and Delegate Selection, which came to be known informally as the McGovern-Fraser Commission. The purpose of the commission was to design rules intended to broaden participation in the Democratic primary process. In particular, the new rules emphasized the need for broader representation of traditionally minority groups and other groups that had been shut out of the convention process. The commission eventually met seventeen times between 1969 and 1972 and ultimately produced a report called "Mandate for Reform." The rules set by the commission would go into effect for the 1972 primary season.

SOURCE: Senator George McGovern (SD), "Mandate for Reform," *Congressional Record*, part 2, 92 (September 22, 1971), 32915–32917. https://www.govinfo.gov/content/pkg/GPO-CRECB-1971-pt25/pdf/GPT-CRECB-1971-pt25-3-3.pdf.

Part II—The Guidelines

A–1 Discrimination on the basis of race, color, creed, or national origin

The 1964 Democratic National Convention adopted a resolution which conditioned the seating of delegations at future conventions on the assurance that discrimination in any State Party affairs on the grounds of race, color, creed or national origin did not occur.... In 1966, the Special Equal Rights Committee, which had been created in 1964, adopted six ... antidiscrimination standards—designated as the "six basic elements"—for the State Parties to meet....

These actions demonstrate the intention of the Democratic Party to ensure a full opportunity for all minority group members to participate in the delegate selection process....

A–2 Discrimination on the basis of age or sex

The Commission believes that discrimination on the grounds of age or sex is inconsistent with full and meaningful opportunity to participate in the delegate selection process. Therefore, the Commission requires State Parties to eliminate all vestiges of discrimination on these grounds. Furthermore, the Commission requires State Parties to overcome the effects of past discrimination by affirmative steps to encourage representation on the national delegation of young people ... and women in reasonable relationship to their presence in the population of the State....

A–5 Existence of party rules

In order for rank-and-file Democrats to have a full and meaningful opportunity to participate in the delegate selection process, they must have access to the substantive and procedural rules which govern the process. In some States the process is not regulated by law or rule, but by resolution of the State Committee and by tradition. In other States, the rules exist, but generally are inaccessible. In still others, rules and laws regulate only the formal aspects of the selection process (e.g., date and place of the State convention) and leave to Party resolution or tradition the more substantive matters (e.g., intrastate apportionment of votes; rotation of alternates; nomination of delegates). The Commission believes that any of these arrangements is inconsistent with the spirit of the Call in that they permit excessive discretion on the part of Party officials, which may be used to deny or limit full and meaningful opportunity to participate. Therefore, the Commission requires State Parties to adopt and make available readily accessible statewide Party rules and statutes which prescribe the State's delegate selection process with sufficient details and clarity....

B–2 Clarity of purpose

An opportunity for full participation in the delegate selection process is not meaningful unless each Party member can clearly express his preference for candidates for delegates to the National Convention, or for those who will select such delegates. In many States, a Party member who wishes to affect the selection of the delegates must do so by voting for delegates or Party officials who will engage in many activities unrelated to the delegate selection process. Whenever other Party business is mixed, without differentiation, with the delegate selection process, the Commission requires State Parties to make it clear to voters how they are participating in a process that will nominate their Party's candidate for President. Furthermore, in States which employ a convention or committee system; the Commission requires State Parties to clearly designate the delegate selection procedures as distinct from other Party business.

B–6 Adequate representation of minority views on presidential candidates at each stage in the delegate selection process

The Commission believes that a full and meaningful opportunity to participate in the delegate selection process is precluded unless the presidential preference of each Democrat is fairly represented at all levels of the process. Therefore, the Commission urges each State Party to adopt procedures which will provide fair representation of minority views on presidential candidates and recommends that the 1972 Convention adopt a rule requiring State Parties to provide for the representation of minority views to the highest level of the nominating process. The Commission believes that there are at least two different methods by which a State Party can provide for such representation. First, in at-large elections it can divide delegate votes among presidential candidates in proportion to their demonstrated strength. Second, it can choose delegates from fairly apportioned districts no larger than congressional districts.

C–4 Premature delegate selection (timeliness)

The 1968 Convention adopted language adding to the Call to the 1972 Convention the requirement that the delegate selection process much begin within the calendar year of the Convention. In many States, Governors, State Chairmen, State, district and county committees who are chosen before the calendar year of the Convention, select—or choose agents to select—the delegates. These practices are inconsistent with the Call. The Commission believes that the 1968 Convention intended to prohibit any untimely procedures which have any direct bearing on the process by which National Convention delegates are selected. The process by which delegates are nominated is such a procedure. Therefore, the Commission requires State Parties to prohibit any practices by which official elected or appointed before the calendar year choose nominating committees or propose or endorse a slate of delegates—even when the possibility for a challenge to such slate or committee is provided. When State law controls, the Commission requires State Parties to make all feasible efforts to repeal, amend, or modify such laws to accomplish the stated purposes.

First Inaugural Address

President Ronald Reagan

January 20, 1981

B efore Reagan took office in 1981, only three Republican presidents had occu-
pied the White House since the New Deal. Unlike those previous presidents,
however, Reagan became the embodiment of the conservative movements of the
1960s. Reagan was the fulfillment of a right-wing revolt that had begun with the
candidacy of Barry Goldwater against the reigning liberal orthodoxy. Reagan
campaigned tirelessly in 1980, promising to get government off people's backs. He
compared government to a free-spending child, suggesting that a parent can be
less generous or cut the child's allowance. The time had come to cut the government's allowance.

Reagan picked up the endorsement of several major Protestant leaders,
adding white evangelicals to his coalition. In addition, he made inroads among
right-to-life Catholics who flocked to Reagan in heavy numbers.

Expressing ideas in simple and folksy ways endeared Reagan to the masses
and allowed him to explain conservative ideas to a large audience. Reagan asked
voters the simple question of whether they were better off today than they were
four years ago. Reagan's message of conservatism, along with public dissatisfaction
with the Carter administration, placed him in the White House. There he brought
together several burgeoning social movements, such as the neo-conservatives and
the supply-siders.[1] After Reagan's nomination, he supported Republicans of all
stripes running for congressional and state office and thus created a large tent
for Republicans to unite under. The result was a cohesive Republican Party built
around a set of conservative ideas and Reagan's personality.

SOURCE: Ronald Reagan, "Inaugural Address," January 20, 1981. Online by Gerhard Peters
and John T. Woolley, *The American Presidency Project.* https://www.presidency.ucsb.edu/
node/246336.

---

[1] Neo-conservatives were former New Deal liberals who had become disenchanted
with the Great Society and had made a shift to conservatism. Supply-siders were
conservative economists who held that cutting taxes was a sure route to economic
prosperity.

To a few of us here today this is a solemn and most momentous occasion, and yet in the history of our nation it is a commonplace occurrence. The orderly transfer of authority as called for in the Constitution routinely takes place, as it has for almost two centuries, and few of us stop to think how unique we really are. In the eyes of many in the world, this every-4-years ceremony we accept as normal is nothing less than a miracle.

Mr. President, I want our fellow citizens to know how much you did to carry on this tradition. By your gracious cooperation in the transition process, you have shown a watching world that we are a united people pledged to maintaining a political system which guarantees individual liberty to a greater degree than any other, and I thank you and your people for all your help in maintaining the continuity which is the bulwark of our Republic.

The business of our nation goes forward. These United States are confronted with an economic affliction of great proportions. We suffer from the longest and one of the worst sustained inflations in our national history. It distorts our economic decisions, penalizes thrift, and crushes the struggling your and the fixed-income elderly alike. It threatens to shatter the lives of millions of our people.

Idle industries have cast workers into unemployment, human misery, and personal indignity. Those who do work are denied a fair return for their labor by a tax system which penalizes successful achievement and keeps us from maintaining full productivity.

But great as our tax burden is, it has not kept pace with public spending. For decades we have piled deficit upon deficit, mortgaging our future and our children's future for the temporary convenience of the present. To continue this long trend is to guarantee tremendous social, cultural, political, and economic upheavals.

You and I, as individuals, can, by borrowing, live beyond our means, but for only a limited period of time. Why, then, should we think that collectively, as a nation, we're not bound by that same limitation? We must act today in order to preserve tomorrow. And let there be no misunderstanding: We are going to begin to act, beginning today.

The economic ills we suffer have come upon us over several decades. They will not go away in days, weeks, or months, but they will go away. They will go away because we as Americans have the capacity now, as we've had in the past, to do whatever needs to be done to preserve this last and greatest bastion of freedom.

In this present crisis, government is not the solution to our problem; government is the problem. From time to time we've been tempted to believe that society has become too complex to be managed by self-rule, that government by an elite group is superior to government for, by, and of the people. Well, if no one among us is capable of governing himself, then who among us has the capacity to govern someone else? All of us together, in and out of government, must bear the burden. The solutions we seek must be equitable, with no one group singled out to pay a higher price.

We hear much of special interest groups. Well, our concern must be for a special interest group that has been too long neglected. It knows no sectional boundaries or ethnic and racial divisions, and it crosses political party lines. It is made up of men and women who raise our food, patrol our streets, man our mines and factories, teach our children, keep our homes, and heal us when we're sick—professionals, industrialists, shopkeepers, clerks, cabbies, and truckdrivers. They are, in short, "We the people," this breed called Americans.

Well, this administration's objective will be a healthy, vigorous, growing economy that provides equal opportunities for all Americans with no barriers born of bigotry or discrimination. Putting America back to work means putting all Americans back to work. Ending inflation means freeing all Americans from the terror of runaway living costs. All must share in the productive work of this "new beginning," and all must share in the bounty of a revived economy. With the idealism and fair play which are the core of our system and our strength, we can have a strong and prosperous America, at peace with itself and the world.

So, as we begin, let us take inventory. We are a nation that has a government—not the other way around. And this makes us special among the nations of the Earth. Our government has no power except that granted it by the people. It is time to check and reverse the growth of government, which shows signs of having grown beyond the consent of the governed.

It is my intention to curb the size and influence of the Federal establishment and to demand recognition of the distinction between the powers granted to the Federal Government and those reserved to the States or to the people. All of us need to be reminded that the Federal Government did not create the States; the States created the Federal Government.

Now, so there will be no understanding, it's not my intention to do away with government. It is rather to make it work—work with us, not over us; to stand by our side, not ride on our back. Government can and must provide opportunity, not smother it; foster productivity, not stifle it.

...Now, I have used the words "they" and "their" in speaking of these heroes. I could say "you" and "your," because I'm addressing the heroes of whom I speak—you, the citizens of this blessed land. Your dreams, your hopes, your goals are going to be the dreams, the hopes, and the goals of this administration, so help me God.

We shall reflect the compassion that is so much a part of your makeup. How can we love our country and not love our countrymen; and loving them, reach out a hand when they fall, heal them when they're sick, and provide opportunity to make them self-sufficient so they will be equal in fact and not just in theory?

Can we solve the problems confronting us? Well, the answer is an unequivocal and emphatic "yes." To paraphrase Winston Churchill, I did not take the oath I've just taken with the intention of presiding over the dissolution of the world's strongest economy.

In the days ahead I will propose removing the roadblocks that have slowed our economy and reduced productivity. Steps will be taken aimed at restoring the balance between the various levels of government. Progress may be slow, measured in inches and feet, not miles, but we will progress. It is time to reawaken this industrial giant, to get government back within its means, and to lighten our punitive tax burden. And these will be our first priorities, and on these principles there will be no compromise.

On the eve of our struggle for independence a man who might have been one of the greatest among the Founding Fathers Dr. Joseph Warren, president of the Massachusetts Congress, said to his fellow Americans, "Our country is in danger, but not to be despaired of.... On you depend the fortunes of America. You are to decide the important questions upon which rests the happiness and the liberty of millions yet unborn. Act worthy of yourselves."

... I'm told that tens of thousands of prayer meetings are being held on this day, and for that I'm deeply grateful. We are a nation under God, and I believe God intended for us to be free. It would be fitting and good, I think, if on each Inaugural Day in future years it should be declared a day of prayer.

This is the first time in our history that this ceremony has been held, as you've been told, on this West Front of the Capitol. Standing here, one faces a magnificent vista, opening up on this city's special beauty and history. At the end of this open mall are those shrines to the giants on whose shoulders we stand.

Directly in front of me, the monument to a monumental man, George Washington, father of our country. A man of humility who came to greatness reluctantly. He led America out of revolutionary victory into infant nationhood. Off to one side, the stately memorial to Thomas Jefferson. The Declaration of Independence flames with his eloquence. And then, beyond

the Reflecting Pool, the dignified columns of the Lincoln Memorial. Who-
ever would understand in his heart the meaning of America will find it in
the life of Abraham Lincoln.

Beyond those monuments to heroism is the Potomac River, and on the
far shore the sloping hills of Arlington National Cemetery, with its row upon
row of simple white markers bearing crosses or Stars of David. They add up
to only a tiny fraction of the price that has been paid for our freedom....

Republican Contract with America

Republican National Committee

September 27, 1994

*T*he Contract with America was a document released for the 1994 midterm elections by the Republican Party explaining what the party would do if it won the majority in Congress. The contract, written by Newt Gingrich and Dick Armey, borrowed from a State of the Union address written by Ronald Reagan years earlier. Additional input was provided by the Heritage Foundation, a conservative think tank that dealt primarily with public policy issues and had been working on many of the contract's proposals for several years.

The document was introduced a month and a half before the election and was approved by all but two of the Republican members of the House. The provisions of the contract proved quite popular with the public even though many people were unfamiliar with the contract itself. Republicans gained fifty-four House seats and nine Senate seats in the elections, and the contract was seen as a success by party leaders. The contract then became a focus of the Republican legislative agenda, denying President Bill Clinton working control of Congress. The contract formed a foundation for Republican policymaking as members of Congress pushed for reducing the size of government, lowering taxes, emphasizing entrepreneurship, establishing tort reform, and bringing about welfare reform. These measures resulted in several important pieces of legislation, none probably more important than welfare reform, which was signed into law by President Clinton. The contract also brought unity and cohesiveness to Republicans, especially in the House of Representatives.

SOURCE: Republican Contract with America, September 27, 1994. https://web.archive.org/web/19990427174200/http://www.house.gov/house/Contract/CONTRACT.html.

As Republican Members of the House of Representatives and as citizens seeking to join that body we propose not just to change its policies, but even more important, to restore the bonds of trust between the people and their elected representatives.

That is why, in this era of official evasion and posturing, we offer instead a detailed agenda for national renewal, a written commitment with no fine print.

This year's election offers the chance, after four decades of one-party control, to bring to the House a new majority that will transform the way Congress works.[1] That historic change would be the end of government that is too big, too intrusive, and too easy with the public's money. It can be the beginning of a Congress that respects the values and shares the faith of the American family.

Like Lincoln, our first Republican president, we intend to act "with firmness in the right, as God gives us to see the right."[2] To restore accountability to Congress. To end its cycle of scandal and disgrace. To make us all proud again of the way free people govern themselves.

On the first day of the 104th Congress, the new Republican majority will immediately pass the following major reforms, aimed at restoring the faith and trust of the American people in their government:

FIRST, require all laws that apply to the rest of the country also apply equally to the Congress;

SECOND, select a major, independent auditing firm to conduct a comprehensive audit of Congress for waste, fraud or abuse;

THIRD, cut the number of House committees, and cut committee staff by one-third;

FOURTH, limit the terms of all committee chairs;

FIFTH, ban the casting of proxy votes in committee;

SIXTH, require committee meetings to be open to the public;

SEVENTH, require a three-fifths majority vote to pass a tax increase;

EIGHTH, guarantee an honest accounting of our Federal Budget by implementing zero base-line budgeting.

Thereafter, within the first 100 days of the 104th Congress, we shall bring

---

[1] Republicans had not controlled both houses of Congress for over four decades, and Republican leaders promised to reshape the congressional landscape, from leadership to composition of committees.

[2] From Lincoln's second inaugural address.

to the House Floor the following bills, each to be given full and open debate, each to be given a clear and fair vote and each to be immediately available this day for public inspection and scrutiny.

THE FISCAL RESPONSIBILITY ACT: A balanced budget/tax limitation amendment and a legislative line-item veto to restore fiscal responsibility to an out- of-control Congress, requiring them to live under the same budget constraints as families and businesses.

THE TAKING BACK OUR STREETS ACT: An anti-crime package including stronger truth-in- sentencing, "good faith" exclusionary rule exemptions, effective death penalty provisions, and cuts in social spending from this summer's "crime" bill to fund prison construction and additional law enforcement to keep people secure in their neighborhoods and kids safe in their schools.

THE PERSONAL RESPONSIBILITY ACT: Discourage illegitimacy and teen pregnancy by prohibiting welfare to minor mothers and denying increased AFDC for additional children while on welfare, cut spending for welfare programs, and enact a tough two-years-and-out provision with work requirements to promote individual responsibility.

THE FAMILY REINFORCEMENT ACT: Child support enforcement, tax incentives for adoption, strengthening rights of parents in their children's education, stronger child pornography laws, and an elderly dependent care tax credit to reinforce the central role of families in American society.

THE AMERICAN DREAM RESTORATION ACT: A $500 per child tax credit, begin repeal of the marriage tax penalty, and creation of American Dream Savings Accounts to provide middle class tax relief.

THE NATIONAL SECURITY RESTORATION ACT: No U.S. troops under U.N. command and restoration of the essential parts of our national security funding to strengthen our national defense and maintain our credibility around the world.

THE SENIOR CITIZENS FAIRNESS ACT: Raise the Social Security earnings limit which currently forces seniors out of the work force, repeal the 1993 tax hikes on Social Security benefits and provide tax incentives for private long-term care insurance to let Older Americans keep more of what they have earned over the years.

THE JOB CREATION AND WAGE ENHANCEMENT ACT: Small business incentives, capital gains cut and indexation, neutral cost recovery, risk assessment/cost-benefit analysis, strengthening the Regulatory Flexibility Act and unfunded mandate reform to create jobs and raise worker wages.

THE COMMON SENSE LEGAL REFORM ACT: "Loser pays" laws,

reasonable limits on punitive damages and reform of product liability laws to stem the endless tide of litigation.

THE CITIZEN LEGISLATURE ACT: A first-ever vote on term limits to replace career politicians with citizen legislators.

Further, we will instruct the House Budget Committee to report to the floor and we will work to enact additional budget savings, beyond the budget cuts specifically included in the legislation described above, to ensure that the Federal budget deficit will be less than it would have been without the enactment of these bills.

Respecting the judgment of our fellow citizens as we seek their mandate for reform, we hereby pledge our names to this Contract with America.

Green Party Platform 2000

Platform Committee

June 25, 2000

T*he Green Party of the United States was formed in 2001 as a product of the Association of State Green Parties, which had been in existence since 1996. Like the state organizations, the national party pledged to use the political process to promote a wide-ranging list of causes, including environmentalism, social justice, gender equality, LGBT rights, pacifism, and anti-racism. In many respects, the Greens seemed to reflect the ideals of the Great Society, though with a stronger emphasis on pacifism, LGBT rights, and environmentalism. What stood out the most for the Greens was their insistence on campaign finance reform and the need to get big money out of American politics. From the Greens' perspective, money bought elections, plain and simple, and this reality undermined the principles of democracy and fairness in elections.*

At first the organization did not garner much attention from the electorate. That changed with the election of 2000, when the Greens put forward a ticket featuring consumer advocate Ralph Nader for president and Winona LaDuke as vice president. Their showing was not spectacular, taking only 2.7% of the popular vote. However, because the election between the major party candidates, Bush and Gore, came down to a few hundred votes in Florida, angry Democrats accused Nader of siphoning off votes from Gore that would have given him the victory. Nader denied this interpretation of the results, and subsequent studies have downplayed Nader's significance in Gore's loss.

Despite its meager showing in the election of 2000, the Green Party was able to achieve ballot status in many new states. This proved that popular discontent with the two major political parties still resonated in America, and third parties hoped to tap into that discontent and translate it into viable electoral outcomes. The Greens did not succeed in capturing much of the popular vote, and more importantly won no electoral votes, but what success they did have spoke to undercurrents that ran through America, rejecting the traditional two-party options.

SOURCE: "Official Green Party Platform, as adopted at the National Nominating Convention" (Denver, CO: June 24, 2000), 3–5. https://gpus.org/wp-content/uploads/2015/12/platform_2000.pdf.

GREEN KEY VALUES

1. GRASSROOTS DEMOCRACY

Every human being deserves a say in the decisions that affect their lives and not be subject to the will of another. Therefore, we will work to increase public participation at every level of government and to ensure that our public representatives are fully accountable to the people who elect them. We will also work to create new types of political organizations which expand the process of participatory democracy by directly including citizens in the decision-making process.

2. SOCIAL JUSTICE AND EQUAL OPPORTUNITY

All persons should have the rights and opportunity to benefit equally from the resources afforded us by society and the environment. We must consciously confront in ourselves, our organizations, and society at large, barriers such as racism and class oppression, sexism and homophobia, ageism and disability, which act to deny fair treatment and equal justice under the law.

3. ECOLOGICAL WISDOM

Human societies must operate with the understanding that we are part of nature, not separate from nature.

   We must maintain an ecological balance and live within the ecological and resource limits of our communities and our planet. We support a sustainable society which utilizes resources in such a way that future generations will benefit and not suffer from the practices of our generation. To this end we must practice agriculture which replenishes the soil; move to an energy efficient economy; and live in ways that respect the integrity of natural systems.

4. NONVIOLENCE

It is essential that we develop effective alternatives to society's current patterns of violence. We will work to demilitarize, and eliminate weapons of mass destruction, without being naive about the intentions of other governments.

   We recognize the need for self-defense and the defense of others who are in helpless situations. We promote non-violent methods to oppose practices and policies with which we disagree, and will guide our actions toward lasting personal, community and global peace.

5. DECENTRALIZATION

Centralization of wealth and power contributes to social and economic injustice, environmental destruction, and militarization. Therefore, we support a restructuring of social, political and economic institutions away from a system which is controlled by and mostly benefits the powerful few, to a democratic, less bureaucratic system. Decision-making should, as much as possible, remain at the individual and local level, while assuring that civil rights are protected for all citizens.

6. COMMUNITY-BASED ECONOMICS AND ECONOMIC JUSTICE

We recognize it is essential to create a vibrant and sustainable economic system, one that can create jobs and provide a decent standard of living for all people while maintaining a healthy ecological balance. A successful economic system will offer meaningful work with dignity, while paying a "living wage" which reflects the real value of a person's work.

Local communities must look to economic development that assures protection of the environment and workers' rights; broad citizen participation in planning; and enhancement of our "quality of life." We support independently owned and operated companies which are socially responsible, as well as co-operatives and public enterprises that distribute resources and control to more people through democratic participation.

7. FEMINISM AND GENDER EQUITY

We have inherited a social system based on male domination of politics and economics. We call for the replacement of the cultural ethics of domination and control with more cooperative ways of interacting that respect differences of opinion and gender. Human values such as equity between the sexes, interpersonal responsibility, and honesty must be developed with moral conscience. We should remember that the process that determines our decisions and actions is just as important as achieving the outcome we want....

I. DEMOCRACY

Democracy must empower all citizens to:

- obtain timely, accurate information from their government;
- communicate such information and their judgments to one another through modern technology;
- band together in civic associations in pursuit of a prosperous, just and free society.

The separation of ownership of major societal assets from their control permits the concentration of power over such assets in the hands of the few who control rather than in the hand of the many who own. The owners of the public lands, pension funds, savings accounts, and the public airwaves are the American people, who have essentially little or no control over their pooled assets or their commonwealth.

A growing and grave imbalance between the often-converging power of Big Business, Big Government and the citizens of this country has seriously damaged our democracy.

Corporations have perfected socializing their losses while they capitalize on their profits.

It's time to end "corporate welfare" as we know it. The power of "civic action" is an antidote to abuse. As we look at the dismantling of democracy by the corporatization of society, we need to rekindle the democratic flame. As voter citizens, taxpayers, workers, consumers and shareholders, we need to exercise our rights and, as Jefferson urged, counteract the "excesses of the monied interests."

A. POLITICAL REFORM

1. The Green Party, proposes a COMPREHENSIVE POLITICAL REFORM AGENDA calling for real reform, accountability, and responsiveness in government.

2. Political debate, public policy, and legislation should be judged on its merits, not on the quid pro quo of political barter and money.

3. We propose comprehensive CAMPAIGN FINANCE REFORM, including caps on spending and contributions, at the national and state level, and/or full public financing of elections" to remove undue influence in political campaigns.

4. We will work to ban or greatly limit POLITICAL ACTION COM-MITTEES[1] and restrict SOFT MONEY contributions.

5. We support significant lobbying regulation, strict rules that disclose the extent of political lobbying via "gifts" and contributions. Broad-based reforms of government operations, with congressional reorganization and ETHICS LAWS, must be instituted. At every level of government, we support "Sunshine Laws"[2] that open up the political system to access by ordinary citizens.

6. We recognize individual empowerment, full citizen participation, and PROPORTIONAL REPRESENTATION as the foundation of an effective and PLURALISTIC[3] democracy.

7. We demand choices in our political system. This can be accomplished by proportional representation voting systems such as: 1) Choice Voting (which is candidate-based) 2) Mixed Member Voting (which combines with district representation) ; and/or 3) Party List (which is party based), and semi-proportional voting systems such as: 1) Limited Voting and 2) Cumulative Voting. All are used throughout the free world and by U.S. businesses, and community and non-profit groups to increase democratic representation. We call on local governments to lead the way toward more electoral choice and broader representation.

8. We believe in MAJORITY RULE. Accordingly, we call for the use of INSTANT RUNOFF VOTING[4] in chief executive races (mayor, governor, president, etc.) where voters can rank their favorite candidates (1,2,3, etc.) to guarantee that the winner has majority support and that voters aren't relegated to choosing between the "lesser of two evils."

9. We believe in MULTI-PARTY DEMOCRACY (for partisan elections) as the best way to guarantee majority rule, since more people will have representation at the table where policy is enacted.

10. The Electoral College is an 18th century anachronism. We call for a constitutional amendment abolishing the Electoral College and providing

---

[1] An organization that raises money privately to influence elections or legislation.

[2] Laws requiring certain proceedings of government to be open to the public.

[3] Relating to a system where two or more groups are sources of authority.

[4] An electoral system where voters rank candidates in order of preference. If no candidate gets a majority, the candidate with the fewest number of first-preference rankings is eliminated and these votes are redistributed. The process is repeated until one candidate achieves a majority.

for the direct election of the president by Instant Runoff Voting. Until that time, we call for a proportional allocation of delegates in state primaries."

11. We encourage building alternative, grassroots institutions that support participatory and direct democracy at the local level. Political reform goes beyond elected politics, ultimately residing in choices each of us makes in our own lives.

12. Using our voice to help others find their voice, a national Green Party should spring from many sources: state and local Green Party electoral efforts, individual efforts, political involvement and direction at every level. As Greens, we look toward forming bioregional confederations to coordinate regional issues based on natural and ecosystem boundaries instead of traditional political ones.

B. POLITICAL PARTICIPATION

1. Greens advocate direct democracy as a response to local needs and issues, where all concerned citizens can discuss and decide questions that immediately affect their lives, such as land use, parks, schools and community services. We would decentralize many state functions to the county and city level and seek expanded roles for neighborhood boards and associations.

2. We call for more flexibility by states and local decision-making.

3. We advocate maintaining and enhancing federal guarantees in the areas of civil rights protections, environmental safeguards, and social "safety net" entitlements.

4. We endorse and advocate citizen rights to INITIATIVE, REFERENDUM and RECALL.[5] We believe that these tools of democracy should not be for sale to the wealthy who pay for signatures to buy their way onto the ballot. Therefore we call for a certain percentage of signatures gathered to come from volunteer collectors.

5. We call for citizen control of REDISTRICTING processes and moving the "backroom" apportionment process into the public light. Minority representation must be protected and secured in order to protect minority rights.

6. We will act to broaden voter participation and BALLOT ACCESS,

---

[5] The initiative is the right of voters to initiate legislative action. The referendum allows voters to vote on a single political question which has been referred to them for decision. The recall allows voters to vote an elected official out of office before their term of office is up.

urging UNIVERSAL VOTER REGISTRATION and an ELECTION DAY HOLIDAY.

7. We believe that a binding "None of the Above" option on the ballot should be considered.

8. We believe that providing free television and mail under reasonable conditions for every qualified statewide, congressional, presidential candidate and party can move the political process toward increased participation.

9. We support statehood for the District of Columbia. The residents of D.C. must have the same rights as all other U.S. citizens to govern themselves and to be represented in both houses of Congress.

10. Individual participation in the life of our local community—in community projects and through personal, meaningful, voluntary activity—is also political and vital to the health of community.

11. We support citizen involvement at all levels of the decision-making process and hold that DIRECT ACTION can be an effective tool where peaceful democratic activism is appropriate. We support the right to non-violent direct action that supports green values. We call for the implementation of Children's Parliaments, whereby representatives elected by students to discuss, debate and make proposals to their city councils and school boards....

Report on Presidential Nomination Timing and Scheduling

Price-Herman Commission

December 10, 2005

I*n 2005, Democrats confronted the growing problem of "frontloading," which refers to states scheduling their primaries earlier and earlier in the primary season to gain greater exposure and attention from the candidates. Frontloading made the nomination process lengthier and more costly, and it weakened candidates by dragging the process out over a longer period of time. In a way, this problem was a natural result of the McGovern-Fraser Commission Report (Document 33), which, among other things, emphasized the use of the primaries by states in the nominating process. Without establishing a national primary,[1] it was inevitable that states would start vying to vote earlier and earlier in the primary process.*

Traditionally, Iowa and New Hampshire have always been allowed to go first in the primary schedule. In 2003, the Michigan Democratic Party objected to this custom and announced plans to hold their primary on the same day as New Hampshire's. Michigan eventually backed down and abandoned its proposal, but not until the Democratic National Committee agreed to review the schedule of primaries for the 2008 election. A commission was then established to study the scheduling and arrangement of Democratic primaries and caucuses, with the co-chairs being David Price, Representative from North Carolina, and Alexis Herman, who had served as secretary of labor under Bill Clinton. The commission held five public meetings and then submitted its report on December 10, 2005. Even with the report, disputes over the ordering and sequence of primaries would not end, and the controversy over which states vote when continues to this day.

SOURCE: "Report of the Commission on Presidential Nomination Timing and Scheduling," Democratic National Committee, December 10, 2005, 40–45. http://a9.g.akamai.net/7/9/8082/v001/democratic1.download.akamai.com/8082/pdfs/20051215_commission final.pdf.

---

[1] A primary where all the states vote on the same day.

Findings and Recommendations

Pre-Window Period[2]

The questions considered by the Commission with respect to the pre-window period, initially, were whether any contests should be permitted within that period; if so, whether the Iowa caucuses and New Hampshire primary should be designated in the rules; whether other state contests should be allowed to take place within that period; and, if so, how many and when. The Commission examined and discussed a number of different scenarios and alternatives relative to these questions.

With respect to these issues, the Commission found that:

There was consensus among its members that the goal of the nominating process should be to produce the best and strongest Democratic presidential nominee; and that that goal is best achieved by devising a system that gives Democratic candidates an opportunity to present themselves and their views to a broad range of voters and gives voters an opportunity to see, hear and question the candidates and measure them against one another.

Commission members understand and appreciate the valuable role the Iowa caucuses and New Hampshire primary have played in the Democratic nominating process over many election cycles. These are key swing states whose caucus participants and primary voters are informed and engaged. The process in these states subject candidates to "retail politics" involving extensive face to face discussions with voters in addition to the pervasive influence of money and media. The presentations made on behalf of Iowa and New Hampshire state parties were thoughtful, detailed and persuasive in this regard.

At the same time, a majority of Commission members expressed serious concerns that Iowa and New Hampshire are not fully reflective of the Democratic electorate or the national electorate generally—and therefore do not place Democratic candidates before a representative range of voters in the critical early weeks of the process. First, Iowa and New Hampshire together account for only about 1.4% of the nation's population as of 2004. New Hampshire ranks 41st out of 50 states in population. Together they select a total

---

[2] The window is the period of time in which any state is free to hold its first step in the nominating process, either a presidential preference primary or a caucus. The pre-window refers to the period of time before the opening of the window and is the time when Iowa and New Hampshire have been given exceptions in the Party's rules to hold their contests.

of just 11 of the 540 electors in the Electoral College. Second, Iowa and New Hampshire do not represent the racial and ethnic diversity of the Party or of the Nation. It has been often noted that the African American community is the most loyal constituency of the Party, and that the Hispanic/Latino vote—for which the Republicans competed strongly in 2004—is a growing share of the total electorate and a key to the Party's future. Yet, according to the U.S. Census Bureau 2004 American Community Survey, 2.2% of Iowa's Population is African American and 0.8% of New Hampshire's population is African American, compared to 12.2% for the nation as a whole. In terms of African American population, Iowa ranks 40th out of 50 states and New Hampshire ranks 43rd.

The 2004 Census data indicate that the Hispanic/Latino population of Iowa was 3.7% and that of New Hampshire was 2.1%, compared to 14.2% for the nation as a whole.

Third, these two states alone cannot and do not represent the geographic diversity that is increasingly critical to the future of the Democratic Party. As matters stand, no Western or Southern state has any role in the pre-window period. The Commission heard substantial testimony—from Rep. Solic, from Mr. Pineda, from the Democrats for the West group, from a Nebraska DNC member and others—that the Party has made significant inroads in state and local elections in the Western states, that the Western states are critical to the Party's future, and that it is imperative that Western states be given a greater role in the process. A similar logic applies to the South, where the DNC has given priority to rebuilding State Parties.

Commission members' concerns were reinforced by the testimony of numerous presenters. Dr. Mann believed that the calendar should engage more and different types of Democratic voters who currently, because of the importance given to Iowa and New Hampshire combined with front-loading,[3] do not play an active or consequential role in the process. Dr. Walters suggested that the demographic makeup of Iowa and New Hampshire has disadvantaged minority candidates and minority voters to the point where the process might conceivably be vulnerable to a legal challenge under section 2 of the Voting Rights Act. (At least one commentator agrees, suggesting that the first in the nation status of Iowa and New Hampshire has created legally actionable "underenfranchisement"[4] of African American voters.)

---

[3] The moving of states earlier and earlier in the primary process.
[4] Justin Driver, "Underenfranchisement: Black Voters and the Presidential Nomination Process," *Harvard Law Review* 117, no. 7 (2004): 2318.

From different perspectives, a number of presenters also expressed the view, shared by many Commission members, that the disproportionate influence of Iowa and New Hampshire means that, even apart from considerations of diversity and representation, too few voters, too small a slice of the electorate, truly get to participate in the nominating process in a meaningful way. The League of Women Voters suggested that the front-loaded system with two early important contests "leaves most voters out of the selection process because, simply put, the selection is over before it's really begun. A system and schedule that allows a larger number of voters, as well as party members and officials, to participate would build better support and citizen engagement in the process."[5] Curtis Gans of the Committee for the Study of the American Electorate suggested that because of the importance of the first two contests followed by a truncated schedule, "only a small fraction of either the party electorate or the electorate as a whole gets to participate in the selection process."[6] He noted that, in 2004, only 5% of the eligible electorate cast ballots before the process was declared over.

...Accordingly, the Commission recommends for the 2008 nominating process:

A. That the first caucus be held in Iowa and the first primary be held in New Hampshire.
B. That there be an additional one or two first-tier caucuses between the Iowa caucus and the New Hampshire primary.
C. That following the New Hampshire primary, and prior to the opening of the regular window on February 5, 2008, there be one or two presidential preference primaries.
D. That the Rules and Bylaws Committee select the appropriate date on which the pre-window period shall begin, which date shall under no circumstances be earlier than January 14, 2008.
E. That the Rules and Bylaws Committee determine the states (other than Iowa and New Hampshire) whose contests may occur during the pre-window period, applying the following criteria: racial and ethnic diversity; regional diversity; and economic diversity including union density.

---

[5] Ibid.
[6] From Curtis Gans's testimony at the July 16, 2005, Commission meeting.

Inside the Window Period

The continued front-loading of the nominating process has been steady and inexorable. Not only has the process started ever earlier; it has concluded ever earlier; as increasing percentages of delegates are effectively selected earlier in the process. As noted above, the Hunt Commission found that in 1972, 17% of the delegates had been allocated (bound to a presidential candidate) by mid-April, while in 1976 the comparable percentage was 33% and in 1980, 44%. In 1984, by the end of the first week after the window opened, 40.3% of the delegates had been allocated and by mid-April, 57.4% had been allocated.

In 1992, by the end of the second Tuesday of the window (March 10), 40% of the delegates had been allocated and almost exactly half had been allocated by the end of March. In 1996, by the second Tuesday of the window (March 12) 66.67%, two-thirds, of the delegates had been allocated. In 2004, with the regular window opening earlier, by the second Tuesday in March (March 9), 71.4% of the delegates had been allocated.

... Front-loading, as William Mayer and Andrew Busch argue, "greatly accelerates the voters' decision process and thus makes the whole system less deliberative, less rational, less flexible, and more chaotic.... Voters are forced to reach a final decision about their party's next presidential nominee in a remarkably short period of time.... Equally important, front-loading makes it all but impossible for the voters to reconsider their initial judgment if new information becomes available."[7]

... Specifically, the Commission proposes that:

The calendar be divided into the following four time stages:

Stage I: March 4 through March 17, inclusive
Stage II: March 18 through April 7, inclusive
Stage III: April 8 through April 28, inclusive
Stage IV: April 29 through June 10, inclusive

A state would be awarded additional delegates to the 2008 Democratic National Convention equal to the following percentages, applied to the total number of pledged delegates otherwise allocated by the *Charter* and Call to the Convention, and based on the time period in which the state's first determining step in the delegate selection process is scheduled to occur in 2008:

Stage I: 15 percent
Stage II: 20 percent

---

[7] William G. Mayer and Andrew E. Busch, *The Front-Loading Problem in Presidential Nominations* (Washington, DC: Brookings Institution, 2004), 56, 63.

Stage III: 30 percent

Stage IV: 40 percent

The Commission believes that only a system of strong and meaningful incentives, such as the proposed system outlined above, can mitigate against continued front-loading of the process. In that regard, the Commission suggests that the Rules and Bylaws Committee consider and discuss the issue of whether any system of disincentives (i.e., loss of delegates for moving contests earlier) should be incorporated into the process.

Citizens United v.
Federal Election Commission

January 21, 2010

The *Bipartisan Campaign Reform Act (BCRA), also known as the McCain-Feingold Act, altered the Federal Election Campaign Act to pro-hibit corporations and unions from using their general treasury to fund "election-eering communications." This referred to political advertisements that mention a candidate in any context. The alteration applied thirty days before a primary election and sixty days before a general election. Citizens United, a conservative nonprofit organization, sought to run television commercials to promote its doc-umentary about Hillary Clinton,* Hillary: The Movie, *shortly before the Dem-ocratic primary. This decision, however, ran afoul of the BCRA requirements. Citizens United sought injunctive relief, arguing that BCRA was unconstitutional as it applied to the movie, and that BCRA's disclaimer, disclosure, and reporting requirements were unconstitutional as applied to* Hillary *and the ads promot-ing the film. The district court issued a preliminary injunction but granted the Federal Election Commission summary judgment. For parties, the significance of the decision was to open up sources of funding for political activities, partic-ularly from corporations, which the court held had a First Amendment right to contribute to political campaigns. Critics of the decision argued that it would be much more difficult to regulate the amount of money being funneled into cam-paigns and corporations with deep pockets would be able to influence elections more easily. But parties generally supported the decision and saw new avenues to fund their election activities.*

SOURCE: Citizens United v. Federal Election Commission, 558 U.S. 310 (2010). Legal Infor-mation Institute, Cornell Law School. https://www.law.cornell.edu/supct/html/08-205.ZS.html.

APPEAL FROM THE UNITED STATES DISTRICT COURT FOR THE DISTRICT OF COLUMBIA

No. 08-205. Argued March 24, 2009—Reargued September 9, 2009—Decided January 21, 2010

... In January 2008, appellant Citizens United, a nonprofit corporation, released a documentary (hereinafter *Hillary*) critical of then-Senator Hillary Clinton, a candidate for her party's Presidential nomination. Anticipating that it would make *Hillary* available on cable television through video-on-demand within 30 days of primary elections, Citizens United produced television ads to run on broadcast and cable television. Concerned about possible civil and criminal penalties for violating BCRA, it sought declaratory and injunctive relief, arguing that (1) §441b of BCRA is unconstitutional as applied to *Hillary*; and (2) BCRA's disclaimer, disclosure, and reporting requirements, BCRA §§201 and 311, were unconstitutional as applied to *Hillary* and the ads. The District Court denied Citizens United a preliminary injunction[1] and granted appellee Federal Election Commission (FEC) summary judgment.

Held:

... (a) Although the First Amendment provides that "Congress shall make no law ... abridging the freedom of speech," §441b's prohibition on corporate independent expenditures is an outright ban on speech, backed by criminal sanctions. It is a ban notwithstanding the fact that a PAC[2] created by a corporation can still speak, for a PAC is a separate association from the corporation. Because speech is an essential mechanism of democracy—it is the means to hold officials accountable to the people—political speech must prevail against laws that would suppress it by design or inadvertence. Laws burdening such speech are subject to strict scrutiny, which requires the Government to prove that the restriction "furthers a compelling interest and is narrowly tailored to achieve that interest." This language provides a sufficient framework for protecting the interests in this case. Premised on mistrust of governmental power, the First Amendment stands against attempts to disfavor certain subjects or viewpoints or to distinguish among different speakers, which may be a means to control content. The Government may also commit a constitutional wrong when by law it identifies certain preferred speakers.

---

[1] A court order made in the early stages of a lawsuit that prohibits the parties from doing an act.

[2] An organization that raises money privately to influence elections or legislation.

There is no basis for the proposition that, in the political speech context, the Government may impose restrictions on certain disfavored speakers. Both history and logic lead to this conclusion....

(b) The Court has recognized that the First Amendment applies to corporations, e.g., *First Nat. Bank of Boston v. Bellotti*,[3] 435 U. S. 765, 778, n. 14, and extended this protection to the context of political speech....

... *Bellotti* reaffirmed the First Amendment principle that the Government lacks the power to restrict political speech based on the speaker's corporate identity....

... (2) This reasoning also shows the invalidity of the Government's other arguments. It reasons that corporate political speech can be banned to prevent corruption or its appearance.... While a single *Bellotti* footnote purported to leave the question open, 435 U. S., at 788, n. 26, this Court now concludes that independent expenditures, including those made by corporations, do not give rise to corruption or the appearance of corruption. That speakers may have influence over or access to elected officials does not mean that those officials are corrupt. And the appearance of influence or access will not cause the electorate to lose faith in this democracy....

... (4) Because §441b is not limited to corporations or associations created in foreign countries or funded predominately by foreign shareholders, it would be overbroad even if the Court were to recognize a compelling governmental interest in limiting foreign influence over the Nation's political process....

... (b) The disclaimer and disclosure requirements are valid as applied to Citizens United's ads. They fall within BCRA's "electioneering communication" definition: They referred to then-Senator Clinton by name shortly before a primary and contained pejorative references to her candidacy.... At the very least, they avoid confusion by making clear that the ads are not funded by a candidate or political party. Citizens United's arguments that §311 is underinclusive[4] because it requires disclaimers for broadcast advertisements but not for print or Internet advertising and that §311 decreases the

---

[3] First National Bank of Boston v. Bellotti, 425 U.S. 765 (1978). The Court was asked to decide whether the First Amendment protected the rights of corporations to attempt to influence to outcome of elections. The Court held that the right to influence the outcomes of elections is one of the primary rights the First Amendment was meant to protect. There was no material difference whether this speech came from a person or a corporation.

[4] Excluding something that should be included.

quantity and effectiveness of the group's speech were rejected.... This Court also rejects their contention that §201's disclosure requirements must be confined to speech that is the functional equivalent of express advocacy under *WRTL*'s[5] test for restrictions on independent expenditures.... Disclosure is the less-restrictive alternative to more comprehensive speech regulations.... Citizens United's argument that no informational interest justifies applying §201 to its ads is similar to the argument this Court rejected with regard to disclaimers. Citizens United finally claims that disclosure requirements can chill donations by exposing donors to retaliation, but offers no evidence that its members face the type of threats, harassment, or reprisals that might make §201 unconstitutional as applied....

   (c) For these same reasons, this Court affirms the application of the §§201 and 311 disclaimer and disclosure requirements to *Hillary*....

   Reversed in part, affirmed in part, and remanded.

---

[5] FEC v. Wisconsin Right to Life, Inc., 551 U.S. 449 (2007). The Court held that issue ads may not be banned from the months preceding a primary or general election.

Thematic Table of Contents

The Case against Parties and Party Development

Parties and Managing the Electorate

Third Parties and the Structural Change in Parties

Democratization of Parties

Discussion Questions

1. Publius, *Federalist* 10 (November 22, 1787)

A. Why does Publius equate political parties with factions? Are parties and factions really the same thing according to Publius' definition?

B. Compare what Publius says in Federalist 10 to Madison's statements on parties (Documents 2 and 3). How can Madison's change in tone about parties be explained?

2. James Madison, "Parties" (January 23, 1792)

A. What does Madison mean when he distinguishes natural from artificial parties?

B. Is Madison speaking here as an impartial observer of the party system or as a partisan who is loyal to his political party? (See also Document 3.)

3. James Madison, "A Candid State of Parties" (September 22, 1792)

A. How does Madison describe the difference between the parties in his essay? Is this a fair comparison?

B. Is Madison's view on parties analogous to Van Buren's (Document 9)?

4. Thomas Jefferson, Letter to Philip Mazzei (April 24, 1796)

A. How does Jefferson's letter to Mazzei reflect growing partisan discontent in the nation?

B. Does this growing discontent reflect a natural tendency for nations to break up into parties as Madison suggests (Document 2)?

5. President George Washington, Letter to Thomas Jefferson (July 6, 1796)

A. What does it say about Washington and the type of politician he was that he refused to acknowledge Jefferson's letter?

B. Is Washington's refusal to engage in partisan attacks reminiscent of the kind of representative Madison had in mind in *Federalist* 10 (Document 1)? Is it possible to count on such representatives to always being in charge?

6. President George Washington, Farewell Address (September 19, 1796)

A. What fears does Washington express for the young nation about the dangers posed by parties?

B. Are Washington's fears addressed by Jefferson (Document 7) in trying to bring unity to the political parties?

7. President Thomas Jefferson, First Inaugural Address (March 4, 1801)

A. What does Jefferson mean when he says, "We are all Republicans, we are all Federalists"?

B. Is Jefferson's statement easily reconciled with the kind of party characterization described by Madison (Document 3)?

8. Martin Van Buren, Letter to Thomas Ritchie (January 13, 1827)

A. Why does Van Buren address this letter to Thomas Ritchie? What did he hope to gain from winning Ritchie's confidence?

B. Given Van Buren's view of parties (Document 8), is it fair to say that he was responsible for building the modern Democratic Party?

9. Martin Van Buren, *Autobiography* (c. 1854)

A. Why does Van Buren believe that parties are inseparable from free government?

B. Why does Van Buren have such a different view of political parties than Washington (Document 6)?

10. Abraham Lincoln, "House Divided" Speech (June 16, 1858)

A. What did Lincoln mean when he said, "A house divided against itself cannot stand"?

B. Was Lincoln trying for some sort of statement of unity much like Jefferson did in 1801 (Document 7)?

11. Abraham Lincoln, Letter to Henry Pierce and Others (April 6, 1859)

A. Why did Lincoln believe that the Declaration of Independence forms a common ground for political discourse?

B. Is the breakup of the Democratic Party (Documents 13 and 14) exactly the kind of event that Lincoln was warning about in his letter?

12. Republican Party Platform 1860 (May 17, 1860)

A. How do the Republicans try to frame the issues of 1860? How do they try to temper their abolitionist wing?

B. How does the platform compare with the ideas from Lincoln's "House Divided" Speech (Document 10)?

13. Democratic Party Platform 1860 (Douglas Faction) (June 18, 1860)

A. How does the Douglas faction of the Democratic Party try to navigate the slavery issue in their platform?

B. How does the Douglas faction differ from the Breckinridge faction (Document 14) in terms of the platform stance?

14. Democratic Party Platform 1860 (Breckinridge Faction) (November 6, 1860)

A. Why does the Breckinridge faction of the Democratic Party take the position on slavery that it does?

B. Does the Breckinridge platform represent a rejection of the Declaration of Independence (Document 11)?

15. Victoria Woodhull, "The Coming Woman" (March 29, 1870)

A. Where does Woodhull stand on the major issues of the day?

B. Is Woodhull right to focus on more issues than just women's suffrage (Document 25)?

16. Woodrow Wilson, "Wanted—A Party" (September 1, 1886)

A. How did Woodrow Wilson believe that parties could be made stronger?

B. Do Wilson's ideas have merit given the state of the big city machines (Document 20)?

17. Populist Party Platform 1892 (July 4, 1892)

A. Based on their platform, how would you explain the popularity of the populists in 1892? What were they tapping into about American culture at the time?

B. What are some of the essential differences between the populists and the progressives (Documents 23 and 26)?

18. William Jennings Bryan, "Cross of Gold" Speech (July 9, 1896)

A. If Bryan's speech and his campaign were so popular, why did he lose to McKinley? What does that tell us about the state of American politics at the time?

B. How well did Bryan's speech merge with populist ideas (Document 17)?

19. Robert La Follette, "Peril in the Machine" (February 23, 1897)

A. Why does La Follette believe that parties fall apart into machines? What is the remedy for machine politics?

B. Does La Follette propose remedies that could address the likes of George Washington Plunkitt (Document 20)?

20. George Washington Plunkitt, *Plunkitt of Tammany Hall* (1905)

A. What does George Washington Plunkitt mean by "honest graft"? If this is how big city machines operated in practice, did they deserve to be called corrupt?

B. Do the big city machines give rise to the need for Roosevelt's New Nationalism (Document 22)?

21. Woodrow Wilson, "Party Government in the United States" (1908)

A. Why did Woodrow Wilson want to reform political parties when so many other Progressives wanted to try to abolish them?

B. How do Wilson's views differ from the Progressive Party Platform of 1912 (Document 23)

22. Theodore Roosevelt, "The New Nationalism" (September 1, 1910)

A. What was the New Nationalism and how did it propose to transform American politics?

B. How does the New Nationalism compare with Taft's *Popular Government* (Document 24)?

23. Progressive Party Platform 1912, (November 5, 1912)

A. How do the Progressives differentiate themselves from the major parties in 1912?

B. What are some major differences between the Progressive Party Platform of 1912 and the Progressive Party Platform of 1924 (Document 26)?

24. William Howard Taft, *Popular Government* (1913)

A. Why does Taft oppose direct popular primaries? Do his objections have any merit?

B. How does Taft compare with Roosevelt's New Nationalism speech (Document 22) on the role of progressive reforms?

25. Platform of the National Woman's Party (June 1916)

A. Why does the National Woman's Party choose to focus on only one issue in their platform?

B. Should the National Woman's Party have been more encompassing like the Progressives in 1912 or 1924 (Documents 23 and 26)?

26. Progressive Party Platform 1924 (November 4, 1924)

A. What are some key features of the Progressive Party Platform of 1924?

B. What differentiates the Progressive Party Platform of 1924 from the Progressive Party Platform of 1912 (Document 23)?

27. Franklin Delano Roosevelt, Acceptance Speech (July 2, 1932)

A. Roosevelt promises a "new deal" for the American people in the speech. What does he mean by this?

B. Is Roosevelt's New Deal a fulfillment of Theodore Roosevelt's New Nationalism (Document 22)?

28. President Franklin Delano Roosevelt, Fireside Chat on Primaries (June 24, 1938)

A. Why is it important to Roosevelt that all voters participate in presidential primaries?

B. Is Roosevelt's fireside chat a precursor to the McGovern-Fraser Commission (Document 33)?

29. Platform of the States Rights Democratic Party, August 14, 1948

A. Why does the States Rights Democratic Party believe that the pursuit of civil rights is so destructive to the American republic?

B. Does the States Rights Democratic Party have anything in common with the Breckinridge faction of the Democratic Party (Document 14) from 1860?

30. President Lyndon B. Johnson, "Great Society" Speech (May 22, 1964)

A. What is the Great Society and how can it be seen as an extension of the New Deal?

B. Would FDR (Document 27) have agreed with the direction and scope of Johnson's Great Society?

31. Barry Goldwater, Acceptance Speech (July 16, 1964)

A. How can Goldwater be understood as a reaction to modern liberalism (i.e., regulated markets and the use of government to expand civil and political rights) ushered in by FDR?

B. What distinguishes Goldwater from Wallace (Document 32) as a reactionary against the Great Society?

32. George Wallace, "Speech at Madison Square Garden" (October 24, 1968)

A. Why does Wallace focus on the need to preserve law and order in America as one of the main points in this speech?

B. Does the States Rights Democratic Party (Document 29) anticipate the candidacy of George Wallace in 1968?

33. McGovern-Fraser Commission Report (September 22, 1971)

A. What reforms are proposed by the McGovern-Fraser Commission Report to correct perceived defects in the nomination process? Does the shift to primaries really produce better nominees than conventions? Have these reforms worked?

B. Does the McGovern-Fraser Commission bring to fulfillment the goal of the Progressives (Document 23)?

34. President Ronald Reagan, First Inaugural Address (January 20, 1981)

A. What is the basis of the new conservatism that Reagan brought to American politics with his election?

B. In what ways does Reagan build on the earlier work of Barry Goldwater (Document 31)? Can Reagan's views be seen as an extension of Goldwater's ideas? What new elements does Reagan bring to his articulation of conservatism?

35. Republican Contract with America (September 27, 1994)

A. Do the Republicans present a clear and compelling political agenda?

B. How might we compare the Contract with America with the other party platforms (Documents 12, 13, 14, 17, 23, 25, 26, 29)?

36. Green Party Platform 2000 (June 25, 2000)

A. How do the Greens differentiate themselves from the major political parties?

B. How do the Greens compare with other third-party movements in American history (Documents 23, 25, 26, 29)?

37. Price-Herman Commission Report (December 10, 2005)

A. What is the problem with states moving primaries earlier and earlier in the primary process?

Does the Price-Herman Commission Report enhance earlier reform efforts with the nominating process (Document 33)?

38. Citizens United v. Federal Election Commission (January 21, 2010)

A. Why does the Supreme Court hold that corporations deserve First Amendment protection?

B. How does this ruling compare with the goals of direct democracy and government accountability favored by the Progressives (Document 23)?

Suggestions for Further Reading

Baer, Kenneth S., Reinventing Democrats: The Politics of Liberalism from Reagan to Clinton (Lawrence: University Press of Kansas, 2000).

Ceaser, James, Presidential Selection (Princeton: Princeton University Press, 1979).

Chambers, William Nisbet, Political Parties in a New Nation: The American Experience, 1776–1809 (New York: Oxford University Press, 1963).

Gerring, John, Party Ideologies in America (New York: Cambridge University Press, 1998).

Gould, Lewis L., Grand Old Party (New York: Random House, 2003).

Hofstadter, Richard, The Idea of a Party System: The Rise of Legitimate Opposition in the United States, 1780–1840 (Berkeley: University of California Press, 1969).

Kazin, Michael, The Populist Persuasion: An American History (New York: Basic Books, 1995).

Ladd, Everett Carll, Jr., American Political Parties: Social Change and Political Response (New York: W. W. Norton, 1970).

Maisel, L. Sandy, American Political Parties and Elections: A Very Short Introduction (New York: Oxford University Press, 2007).

Maisel, L. Sandy, and Kara Z. Buckley, Parties and Elections in America: The Electoral Process, 6th ed. (Lanham, Md.: Rowman & Littlefield, 2011).

Mayhew, David, Electoral Realignments: A Critique of an American Genre (New Haven: Yale University Press, 2002).

Milkis, Sidney M., The President and the Parties: The Transformation of the American Party System Since the New Deal (New York: Oxford University Press, 1993).

Reichley, James A., The Life of the Parties: A History of American Political Parties (Lanham, Md.: Rowman & Littlefield, 1992).

Schlesinger, Arthur M., Jr., and Fred L. Israel, History of American Presidential Elections, 1789–2001, vol. 1–11 (Philadelphia: Chelsea House, 2002).

Shefter, Martin, Political Parties and the State: The American Historical Experience (Princeton: Princeton University Press, 1994).

———. *Political Parties and Constitutional Government: Remaking American Democracy* (Baltimore: Johns Hopkins University Press, 1999).

Walton, Mary, *A Woman's Crusade: Alice Paul and the Battle for the Ballot* (New York: St. Martin's, 2010).